...earers, although of diffe...

one thing in common:

the long-sleeve

the sleeve-

...

...tit... pattern, which ...

...squares that resembles ...

...veryone loves a ... ...

...gan. And any one of the...

...would be perfect for you...

someone on your gift list.

Katherine, refined in its sim...

plicity, is always in style—

with or without its ruffle...

knits

THREE WAYS

Mix and Match Design Elements to Create a Custom-Made Sweater

To Julie,
Knit on!
Melissa

knits
THREE WAYS

Mix and Match Design Elements to Create a Custom-Made Sweater

POTTER
CRAFT

MELISSA MATTHAY

Copyright © 2007 by Melissa Matthay

All rights reserved.
Published in the United States by Potter Craft, an imprint of
the Crown Publishing Group, a division of Random House,
Inc., New York.
www.crownpublishing.com
www.clarksonpotter.com
www.pottercraftnews.com

POTTER CRAFT and CLARKSON N. POTTER are
trademarks, and POTTER and colophon are registered
trademarks of Random House, Inc.

Library of Congress Cataloging-in-Publication Data is
available upon request.

ISBN 978-0-307-34564-6

Printed in China

Design by Laura Palese

Photographs by Alan Foreman

10   9   8   7   6   5   4   3   2   1

First Edition

Acknowledgments

There are many people in my life I would like to thank. Those of you know who you are. I am indebted to Sheryl Thies, who got me started publishing my own designs and stuck with me for the first five publications. When I tried to convince her to work on this project, too, she told me, "I gave you your wings—it's time for you to fly on your own." A special thank-you also goes to Adina Klein for her never-ending support. I love you, girl! And last, but not least, thank you to Karen Wilder, who was there from the very beginning.

I wouldn't be the creative lunatic I am without the patience, calm, and understanding of my elder son, Aaron Davis, and the exuberant, enthusiastic drive of my younger son, Dylan Davis. I love you boys. Whatever you do, love what you're doing.

Contents

Introduction

Over the twenty-five years I've been knitting, I have talked to hundreds—if not thousands—of knitters. One common lament is that they aren't able to find patterns that match the sweaters they have in mind to make. Photos in pattern books and knitting magazines may come close, but there's always something that doesn't match up—the knitter doesn't like the yarn or the stitch pattern, the neckline isn't right, the sleeves are too short, the body's too long, or the details are too fussy. I've sat down with countless disgruntled knitters to sketch out designs, work up gauge swatches, and adjust patterns to the knitter's vision.

Eventually, I began to realize that most knitters want the same thing: to design their *own* sweaters, whether they are novices looking for a simple sweater to make for their first post-scarf project, intermediate knitters looking to dabble in design, or experienced knitters searching for new ideas to incorporate into their own designs. And so the idea behind *Knits Three Ways* was born.

With twelve basic sweater patterns and three knitting variations for each—for a total of thirty-six designs—*Knits Three Ways* shows knitters how simple changes in yarn, stitch patterns, and lengths can dramatically transform the look and style of a basic pattern to create new sweaters with entirely different personalities.

The book starts with a "Designing Your Own Sweaters" section that provides basic guidelines for measuring, shaping, and finishing, so that every sweater you knit will turn out precisely as desired. You'll find patterns for a geisha-inspired kimono jacket, a supremely comfy hoodie, a stylish shrug, and many other versatile designs, including classic and new takes on the ever-popular pullover and V-neck cardigan. *Knits Three Ways* also delves into the realms of cables, chevrons, and ribbing; sleeve shapes; ribbon and ruffle embellishments; colorful intarsia knitting; and knitting with lace. Each pattern is shown in three different types of yarn and offers variations on the neckline, sleeves, length, embellishments, and trims to create completely different styles—all from the same basic pattern. Along the way you'll find plenty of knitting tips, helpful hints, and suggestions for still more style variations.

For the intrepid knitter, *Knits Three Ways* opens up a myriad of design options, with clearly written pattern instructions for more predictable results. The only problem you're likely to encounter is deciding which of the designs for pullovers, cardigans, jackets, and tank tops you want to try first.

—Melissa

designing

The beauty of designing your own sweater is that you are not bound to any pattern. You are in control and can do what you choose. You can knit them to be as big or small as you want— you're not limited to manufacturers' sizes. Just know your measurements and decide what you want. In the end, though, you do want a sweater that fits and flatters you. If you have a commercial sweater that fits well, you can use its measurements to determine the size of your hand-knitted garments.

Now that I've said you're not limited to standard sizing, let's examine the standards. To get a well-fitting sweater, there are a few guidelines you should understand. Even if you choose not to use them, it is helpful to know what they are. The following discussion applies to a gauge of 5 stitches or less per inch/2.5 cm. With thicker yarn, you will finish the project faster and be wearing your sweater sooner.

As you consider the possibilities for modifying a sweater pattern, the first piece to consider is the body. Sweaters are knit from the bottom up, and most commercial patterns are a square up to the armhole, which is also the bustline. The shaping is done after the armhole. When you design your own sweaters, you can make simple alterations to the "square" to fashion your piece exactly the way you want it. If you have a great body, you can achieve an hourglass effect by decreasing in and increasing out as much as you would like. Maybe you prefer something more forgiving, like the classic tent shape—if so, you would cast on more stitches at the beginning and decrease at regular intervals as you reach the armhole. On the other hand, all you skinny-legged, big-bosomed apple shapes would start by casting on a smaller number of stitches and increasing up to armhole.

STEP ONE: CHOOSING AND CALCULATING YOUR SLEEVES

Sleeves are a good place to start knitting your sweater. Since the type of sleeve you choose affects the bust measurement of your sweater, you have to make some decisions about the sleeves right away. You can also use the sleeves to double-check your gauge. Since you cast on fewer stitches than for the front or back, it's less painful to rip out if you need to change needles. I prefer to use one of three sleeve shapes: drop sleeve, indented drop, or set in. When using a drop sleeve, plan for the sweater to measure 4 to 8 inches/10 to 20.5 cm larger than your actual bust measurement.

For an indented drop, add 2 to 4 inches/5 to 10 cm to your bust measurement; after the indenting, the sweater should measure 1½ inches/3.8 cm more than your bust. For a set-in sleeve, the sweater should be 1 to 3 inches/2.5 to 7.5 cm larger than your bust. This choice will also affect the length of your sleeves; see pages 12–13 to learn how to find those measurements.

Determining Sleeve Width

Regardless of the kind of sleeve you're knitting—drop, indented drop, or set in—you calculate the sleeve from the cuff to the armhole in the same way. The classic sweater sleeve is narrowest at the wrist and increases in width as it moves up the arm. To determine the width of the sleeve, do the following:

Measure the circumference of your wrist (the distance around) and determine how tight you want your cuffs to fit. (A close-fitting cuff will measure around 7 inches/18 cm; the average cuff measures about 8 inches/20.5 cm.) Multiply that measurement by your gauge. The result is the number of stitches you should cast on.

Next, measure the circumference of your upper arm and decide how tightly you'd like the sleeve to fit. Multiply that number by your gauge; the result is the number of stitches you should have at the top, the widest part of the sleeve.

Subtract the number of stitches at the wrist from the number at the top. This is the total number of stitches you'll need to increase.

Divide the total number of increases in half. Increases are worked evenly on both edges of the sleeves, and this calculation gives you the number of increases you need to work on each sleeve edge to get your desired shaping.

Example:

- Let's say your wrist measurement is 7 inches/18 cm. You want the sleeve to measure 15 inches/ 38 cm at the top, and your gauge is 4 stitches per inch/2.5 cm.
- Multiply your wrist measurement by the gauge to get the number of stitches to cast on: 7 inches/ 18 cm × 4 stitches per inch/2.5 cm = 28 stitches.
- Multiply the sleeve measurement by the gauge to get the final number of stitches: 15 inches/38 cm × 4 stitches per inch/2.5 cm = 60 stitches.
- Subtract the number of stitches at the wrist from the number of stitches at the top: 60 − 28 = 32 stitches to increase over length of sleeve.
- Divide that number in half: 32 ÷ 2 = 16 stitches to increase on each sleeve edge.

Cast on the number of stitches for your wrist and work several inches in whatever edge treatment you prefer: ribbing, garter, seed stitch, or plain stockinette stitch for a rolled edge. When you are ready to begin your increases, follow this simple rule: If your gauge is between five stitches and two stitches to the inch/2.5 cm, increase every fourth row. If your gauge is two stitches or fewer per inch/2.5 cm, increase every sixth row.

Work increases two stitches in from the edge for easier seaming, always on the right side, and always on both edges of the sleeve. An increase row in plain stockinette stitch would look like this: Knit two, increase one, knit until two stitches remain, increase one, knit two. I like to remind beginning knitters that this allows for sipping a glass of wine on the purl back row. However, I also remind knitters that one glass of wine with knitting is fine. Be careful with two. When you pour the third, put away the knitting (and the wine, for that matter!). When you have increased to the desired number of stitches, measure the sleeve and knit until it's as long as you want it.

Drop Sleeve

ARMHOLE DEPTH

For most average- to large-sized women, an armhole depth of 10 inches/25.5 cm is comfortable. Smaller women, however, usually prefer an armhole of 8 or 9 inches/20.5 or 23 cm. Since a drop sleeve fits a straight sleeve top against straight sweater sides, a 10-inch/25.5-cm armhole requires a 20-inch/51-cm sleeve top, 10 inches/25.5 cm each for front and back. If your gauge is 4 stitches to the inch/2.5 cm, that would be 80 stitches at the top of the sleeve.

SLEEVE LENGTH

You'll need a helper to determine the required length of your sleeve. Stand straight with your arms very slightly extended away from your body. Have your helper measure from the back of your neck (at the top of your spine) to your wrist. Now use that number in this formula:

Length of sleeve = neck-to-wrist measurement minus one-half the width of the sweater back

Example:

Your neck-to-wrist measurement is 30 inches/76 cm. The sweater back is 21 inches/53.5 cm wide (divided by 2 equals 10½ inches/26.5 cm). The length of your sleeve is 30 inches/76 cm– 10½ inches/26.5 cm = 19½ inches/49.5 cm.

TOP-OF-SLEEVE SHAPING

With a drop sleeve, there is a considerable bulk of fabric under the arms. To remove a little of this bulk without changing the shape of the armhole, shape the top of the sleeve. Once the desired length of sleeve has been achieved, bind off 2 inches/5 cm worth of stitches at the beginning of the next 6 rows. Then bind off the remaining stitches.

Example:

Using our 10-inch/25.5-cm armhole depth, at 4 stitches per inch/2.5 cm, we have 80 stitches on the needle and have reached 19½ inches/ 49.5 cm. At our gauge, 2 inches/5 cm = 8 stitches. To shape the top of the sleeve, therefore, we bind off 8 stitches at the beginning of the next 6 rows. Bind off the remaining 32 stitches.

tip

For nicer seaming, slip the first stitch of the bind-off row (slip one, knit one, bind off the slipped stitch). The slip is for the first stitch only. Complete the remaining bind-offs using the normal method and complete the row.

Indented Drop Sleeve

ARMHOLE DEPTH

Follow the guidelines for a drop sleeve.

SLEEVE LENGTH

Follow the guidelines for a drop sleeve, adding 2 inches/5 cm.

TOP-OF-SLEEVE SHAPING

Follow the guidelines for a drop sleeve.

Set-In Sleeve

The following sections describe the way to proportion a set-in sleeve.

ARMHOLE DEPTH

The overall depth of the armhole will be the same as for a drop sleeve or indented drop. However, you have to shape the sweater body to fit the sleeve cap. Measure your chest from the inside of your shoulder to the inside of the other shoulder. Many women are 14 or 15 inches/35.5 or 38 cm wide at this point. This measure should be maintained once the armhole is created. When the sweater body is as long as you want it up to the armhole, bind off 1 inch/2.5 cm of stitches at the beginning of the next 2 rows. Over the next 1½ to 2 inches/3.8 to 5 cm, you will want to decrease to reach the measurement between your shoulders.

Example:

Your sweater is 20 inches/51 cm wide, giving you 80 stitches at 4 stitches per inch/2.5 cm. The interior shoulder-to-shoulder measurement is 15 inches/38 cm, or 60 stitches. You need to decrease 20 stitches (80 stitches–60 stitches). Binding off 1 inch/2.5 cm (4 stitches) on each side removes 8 stitches, leaving 12 to decrease. Simply decrease 1 stitch on each side of the next 6 right-side rows and knit until the desired armhole depth is achieved. Also, be sure to see the section on Neck Shaping on pages 14–15.

SLEEVE LENGTH

To determine the length of a set-in sleeve, let your arm hang naturally at your side and measure from your underarm (about at the top of your bra) to your wrist. The average length seems to be about 16 inches/40.5 cm.

TOP-OF-SLEEVE SHAPING

The cap of a set-in sleeve does not mirror the armhole shaping of the body. The cap begins the same way: Once you have achieved the desired sleeve length, bind off 1 inch/2.5 cm of stitches at the beginning of the next 2 rows. Then decrease 1 stitch at each end of the right-side rows until the sleeve cap is 2 inches/5 cm less than armhole depth. Bind off ½ inch/13 mm of stitches at the beginning of the next four rows. Bind off remaining stitches.

Example:

If your sleeve has 60 stitches at the top, with a gauge of 4 stitches to the inch/2.5 cm, you will bind off 4 stitches at the beginning of the first 2 rows after the sleeve is long enough. Assuming a 10-inch/25.5-cm armhole on the sweater, decrease at each end of the right-side rows until the sleeve cap is 5 inches/12.5 cm long. Bind off 2 stitches at the beginning of the next 4 rows. Bind off the remaining stitches.

Making a Vest Armhole

The depth of the armhole for a vest should be an inch or two/2.5 or 5 cm deeper than it would be for a sweater. The extra room allows the vest to hang correctly and accommodate the sleeves of the shirt underneath without pulling in under the arms. A depth of 10 or 11 inches/25.5 or 28 cm is usually about right.

STEP TWO: DETERMINE THE SWEATER LENGTH

Once your sleeves are knit, it is time to move on to the body of your sweater. This you will knit according to the pattern you've chosen and your personal taste, increasing and decreasing as desired to make the body fit more tightly or loosely.

However, there is one general piece of advice that is good to remember for all sweater types: Don't end the sweater at the widest part of your body. Either shorten it up or make it longer.

STEP THREE: SHAPING THE NECK

Necks require shaping, something usually taken care of in the shoulders by steaming and gravity. The straight bind-off omits the laddering that makes for ragged seams, and the bound-off edge acts as a stabilizer.

When working the back of the neck, you will find that many patterns call for stitches to be put on a holder or to be bound off using the three-needle method. While the three-needle bind-off does line up the stitches in an interlocking fashion, neither of these methods provides much stability. For the back of the neck, it is best to work a straight bind-off, followed by firm seaming. This method provides great stabilization in a part of the sweater that takes a lot of stress and stretching.

Crew Neck

On a standard crew-neck sweater, the back neck measurement is 7 inches/18 cm. This is true regardless of the sleeve type. On the front, neck shaping begins 3 inches/7.5 cm lower than it does on the back. If the back measures 21 inches/53.5 cm in length, begin the front neck shaping when the piece measures 18 inches/45.5 cm. The front center bind-off should equal 4 inches/10 cm. If you're making a cardigan, that would be 2 inches/5 cm on each neck edge side.

The front center stitches can be put on a holder if you are going to continue the body pattern into the neck. Since that part of the sweater bears much less of the garment's weight than the shoulders, stabilization is not as important along the front neck edge.

The curved edge decreases should equal 1½ inches/3.8 cm on each side, adding 3 inches/7.5 cm to the 4 inches/10 cm that make up the front center bind-off for a total of 7 inches/18 cm. (This matches the back neck measurement, also 7 inches/18 cm. When binding off, remember to slip the first stitch for a smoother, less ragged edge and to work your decreases 2 stitches from the edge. There will usually be a U-shaped curve. When you are on the right side of the garment you should sl1, k1, psso. For full-fashion detail, k1 or k2, then sl1, k1, psso. For full fashion detail, work to the last 3 or 4 sts, k2tog then k1 or k2.

Example:

The garment front is 20 inches/51 cm wide, or 80 stitches at our gauge of 4 stitches per inch/2.5 cm. The initial front neck bind-off is 16 stitches (4 inches/10 cm × 4 stitches per inch/2.5 cm). A further decrease of 1½ inches/3.8 cm requires decreasing 6 stitches on either side of the neck (1½ inches/3.8 cm × 4 stitches per inch/2.5 cm). Decrease 1 stitch on each side on the next 6 right-side rows. Some knitters prefer to do a second bind-off row of half an inch/13 mm or so before beginning the curve. This is best left to the knitter's preference. Once the neck band is applied, the curve is pulled in, so that little difference is hardly noticeable.

V-Neck

Classic V-neck shaping begins an inch/2.5 cm before the armhole shaping. However, since you are in charge of your knitting, you can start the shaping anywhere you please. Since the neck opening should be 7 inches/18 cm wide and you will be decreasing on both sides of the V, you need to decrease 3½ inches/9 cm on each side. At a gauge of 4 stitches to the inch/2.5 cm, that comes out to 14 decreases on each side. For a classic V-neck, decreasing every 4 rows works well. For a low, narrow V, decrease every 8 rows. For a high, wide V, decrease every other row.

STEP FOUR: FINISHING

At this point, you have knitted your sleeves, the front and back pieces, and you have done the shaping for the neck. The next and final step is to "finish" your sweater. This includes sewing seams and completing the neck and button bands (if necessary).

Sewing Seams

When sewing seams, use a blunt yarn needle and, wherever possible, the same yarn that you used for the sweater. The right side of your work is the side that you will be wearing. If the garment is purl side out, the purl side is your right side. With the edges of the work side by side, put the needle under the strand of yarn between the first stitch and the second stitch and draw the thread through. Put the needle under the same strand on the other side and draw the yarn through. Return to the first side and repeat the process.

Single Crochet

A single crochet is a very nice edge for a base. The formula for a vertical row edge is one single crochet every other row. The formula for the horizontal bind-off edge is one single crochet every 1½ stitches. Go into the stitch, then go in between the next two stitches and repeat across the row.

Picking Up Stitches for Neck and Button Bands

You will have to pick up stitches for the neck band and, if you are knitting a cardigan, for the button bands also. For the neck edge, with the right side of the work facing you, begin at the right shoulder seam and pick up a stitch for every stitch along the back edge. On the vertical front edge, where you are picking up stitches from the ends of rows, you need to adjust for the fact that there is one more row per inch/2.5 cm—in other words, with a gauge of 4 stitches per inch/2.5 cm, you likely have about 5 rows per inch/2.5 cm. Pick up 5 stitches, one per row bar, then skip the sixth. Repeat until you reach the front slope. On the slope, pick up every stitch. By following this formula, you will have eventually distributed the stitches to work a nicely proportioned neck.

If you are knitting a ribbed neck band, use a smaller needle size than you used for the body of the sweater. If you're knitting a pattern stitch, you may have to adjust the number of stitches to make the pattern work. For instance, a k2, p2 rib has a four-stitch repeat. The number of stitches must be evenly divisible by four. The neck band will look much nicer if you pick up stitches according to the formula in the last pattern and then either increase or decrease on your first round to get the proper number.

For the button band, position the work with the right side facing you. Pick up stitches using the vertical row bar formula: your stitch gauge plus one, skip one, and repeat. By following this method, you will have evenly distributed stitches for a button band that neither flares nor pulls in, and you will have the same number of stitches on each button band. Work in pattern.

Making Buttonholes

Determine the size and number of the buttons you want to use. Like the petals of a flower, an odd number seems to be more pleasing than an even one. The size of the button will determine the size of the buttonhole. A ⅝-inch/16-mm button or smaller may not require a buttonhole, as the button can probably slip between the stitches. A 1-inch/2.5-cm button requires a 1-stitch buttonhole. Larger buttons require a 2-stitch buttonhole. Remember that the yarn and the buttonhole will stretch. Keep the buttonhole small enough for the hole to hold the button; too loose, and it won't stay closed.

Buttonhole Method

Determine the desired width of your button band and work the buttonholes one row closer to the pick-up edge than the center. This will provide a stable button band. To determine when to work the buttonholes, use this formula:

Number of stitches in button band—6 stitches—(number of buttons × number of stitches per button) divided by (number of buttonholes—1)

This method will evenly distribute the buttonholes along the band, 3 stitches from the top and bottom. For a 1-stitch buttonhole, *work the number of stitches, yarn over, knit two together; repeat from *. For a two-stitch buttonhole, *work the number of stitches, slip two, pass the first slipped stitch over the second, slip another, pass slipped stitch over last one slipped, put last stitch back on left needle, cast on two stitches; repeat from *. For a larger button, follow the directions for the two-stitch buttonhole, slipping and passing over as many stitches as are required, remembering to cast the same number of stitches back on.

Blocking

Blocking will smooth out most irregularties and help in the final shaping of your garment. Blocking after the garment is completed will also help soften the seams. Set your iron to the highest setting. While it is heating up, wet a hand towel and wring it out. Spread a dry towel on a flat surface, lay the garment on top of it, carefully shaped to the desired measurements, and cover the garment with the wet hand towel. Lower the iron ever so gently as close to the towel as you can without making contact. You will hear the "psstt" and see steam. Never let the weight of the iron touch the garment. If you block too much, you cannot bring the piece back to life, so be sure to work little steps and repeat until you've achieved the desired shape. Then let it dry.

designing WITH YARN

An easy way to individualize a sweater is to combine several strands to make your own custom yarn. You may want to combine yarns as a means of bulking up to achieve a specific gauge or simply to play with color and texture. Your imagination is your only limitation when it comes to combining yarns, so let yourself go wild.

Here are a few simple guidelines to get you started:

Two double-knitting (DK) weight yarns = 3.5 stitches per inch/2.5 cm

Dk plus worsted = 3 stitches per inch/2.5 cm

Two worsted weight yarns = 2.75 stitches per inch/ 2.5 cm

- Combining two solid colors will give a ragg look. The effect will be more pronounced the more the colors contrast with each other.
- Combining a textured or slub yarn with a flat yarn can achieve exciting effects without overwhelming the wearer.
- Combining two or three textured yarns will give you a very different yarn with new depth, but could be too much of a good thing.
- To see how the yarns may combine, pull out about 10 inches/25.5 cm of each of the yarns, twist, and wrap around your finger. I suggest that if you're planning on going into your local yarn shop to pull out all their skeins, bring a box of very good chocolates and please, please pick up after yourself.

WHEN IN DOUBT, SWATCH!

the classic sweater

We think of a classic sweater as being shaped to fit the body,
with set-in sleeves and a round neck. The three versions shown
here differ only slightly, yet each looks completely individual.
Eve has a mock rolled neck, Kenya is loosely knitted with a
textured yarn and a scooped neckline, and Ruby's bodice has a
different yarn and stitch pattern than the yoke and sleeves.

This is the classic
set-in-sleeve sweater
with a rolled mock
turtleneck. It's
named "Eve" because
it is so basic almost
any sweater can be
based on a variation
of it. The simplicity
of the design makes
it fun to accessorize
with a scarf,
brooch, or beads.

Eve

DESIGNER'S NOTES

I chose to knit this one in Lion Brand Cashmere Blend using stockinette stitch. I did a 4-inch/10-cm mock turtle, which could be left up or rolled down, as shown here. The length of the neck in stockinette stitch will determine the size of the roll. If you stockinette stitch for 1½ to 2 inches/3.8 to 5 cm, you get a smaller roll.

There are many other neck options. If you like, you could choose a K1, P1 rib. For a classic crew neck, you would knit in that pattern for 1¼ inches/3 cm. To make a full turtleneck, knit the K1, P1 rib for 7 inches/18 cm.

Remember to bind off loosely in ribbing. Sometimes the best way to make sure that you are binding off loosely is to use needles one or two sizes larger than the needles you were working with.

INSTRUCTIONS

back

With size 10 needles, CO 64 (70, 74, 78) sts. Work even in St st until piece measures 13 (14, 14, 15)"/33 (35.5, 35.5, 38) cm.
SHAPE ARMHOLE: BO 3 sts at beg of next 2 rows, then dec 1 st at each edge every other row 4 (5, 5, 6) times, for 50 (54, 58, 60) sts. Work even until piece measures 20½ (22, 22½, 24)"/52 (56, 57, 61) cm. BO loosely.

front

Work same as back until piece measures 17 (18, 18½, 19)"/43 (45.5, 47, 48.5) cm.
SHAPE NECK: Work 18 (20, 22, 23) sts, join a second ball of yarn and BO center 14 sts; work to end of row. Working both sides at once, BO at each neck edge 3 sts once, then dec 1 st every other row 3 times—12 (14, 16, 17) sts remaining for each shoulder. Work even until piece measures same as back. BO loosely.

sleeves

With size 10 needles, CO 26 (30, 30, 32) sts. Work in St st, and *at the same time*, inc 1 st at each end every 6th row 7 (7, 8, 8) times. *(Note: For better seams, work incs 2 sts in from edges.)* Work even until piece measures 16 (16½, 16½, 17)"/40.5 (42, 42, 43) cm.
SHAPE CAP: BO 3 sts at beg of next 2 rows. Then dec 1 st at each edge every other row 10 (11, 12, 12) times. Then BO 2 sts at beginning of next 4 rows. BO remaining 6 (8, 8, 10) sts.

finishing

Sew shoulder seams.
NECK BAND: With circular needles, pick up and knit 70 (74, 74, 78) sts around neck edge. Join and work in St st for 4"/10 cm. BO all sts *loosely*.
Sew on sleeves. Sew side and sleeve seams (see page 15).

Skill level | EASY

Sizes

SMALL (Medium, Large, Extra-Large) Instructions are given for smallest size, with larger sizes in parentheses. When only one number is given, it applies to all sizes.

Finished Measurements

CHEST 37 (40, 42, 45)"/94 (101.5, 106.5, 114) cm
LENGTH 20½ (22, 22½, 24)"/52 (56, 57, 61) cm

Materials

9 (10, 12, 13) skeins Lion Brand Cashmere Blend (72% merino wool, 14% cashmere, 14% nylon: 1½ oz/40 g; 84 yds/77 m) in #98 Crème

Needles

Size 10 (6 mm) straight and circular, or size needed to obtain gauge

Gauge

14 sts and 18 rows = 4"/10 cm over St st
To save time, take time to check gauge.

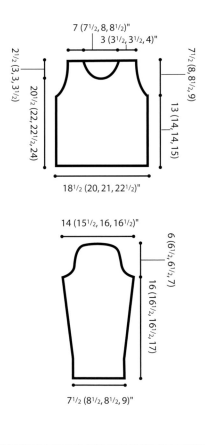

DESIGNER'S NOTES

Those of you who are more self-conscious can knit the complementary yarn all the way through the garment. And you gals who are more daring can do the garment in the slubbed yarn alone.

When you're knitting your yarn more loosely than normal, you'll find it more difficult to take a gauge. Every time you measure, you'll seem to come up with a different number. That's because the piece stretches longer when you hold it up on its needles. What you want to do instead is to lay it on a flat surface, so it doesn't stretch, and pat it down. Using a tape measure, place the 1-inch/2.5-cm mark at the base of your knitting needle and measure. (Don't stretch your work!)

When in doubt about the length, remember that loosely knit garments have a tendency to "grow." In other words, if the desired length of the final product is 24 inches/61 cm, you may want to stop at 23 inches/58.5 cm. The same is true for the neckline. After a lot of wears, you might find that the neckline is getting too big. This is when your crochet hook comes in handy.

Kenya

Kenya has the same classic shape as Eve but with a scooped neckline. It's knitted with a beautiful variegated, slubbed yarn to give the garment a lacy see-through look. To prevent a bra from showing through, a thin complementary yarn is knitted just through the bust area.

Skill level : EASY

Sizes

SMALL (Medium, Large, Extra-Large) Instructions are given for smallest size, with larger sizes in parentheses. When only one number is given, it applies to all sizes.

Finished measurements

CHEST 37 (40, 42, 45)"/94 (101.5, 106.5, 114) cm
LENGTH 20½ (22, 22½, 24)"/52 (56, 57, 61) cm

Materials

MC: 3 (4, 4, 5) skeins Great Adirondack Yarns Cyclone (100% rayon: 4 oz/110 g; 187 yds/160 m) in Leopard
CC: 1 skein Tahki Stacy Charles Filatura Di Crosa Millefili Fine (100% cotton: 1¾ oz/50 g; 137 yds/125 m) in #61 Black

Needles

Size 10 (6 mm) or size needed to obtain gauge
Size H-8 (5 mm) crochet hook (optional)

Gauge

14 sts and 18 rows = 4"/10 cm over St st
To save time, take time to check gauge.

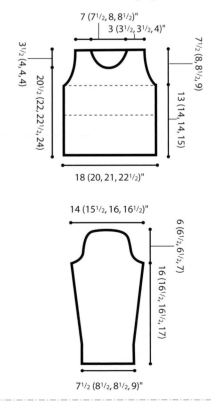

INSTRUCTIONS

back

With size 10 needles, CO 64 (70, 74, 78) sts. Work even in reverse St st until piece measures 9 (10, 10½, 11)"/23 (25.5, 26.5, 28) cm. Join CC. Work with both strands of yarn for 5 (5½, 6, 6½)"/12.5 (14, 15, 16.5) cm. Cut CC. Work even *at the same time* until piece measures 13 (14, 14, 15)"/33 (35.5, 35.5, 38) cm.
SHAPE ARMHOLE: BO 3 sts at beg of next 2 rows, then dec 1 st at each edge every other row 4 (5, 5, 6) times, for 50 (54, 58, 60) sts. Work even until piece measures 20½ (22, 22½, 24)"/ 52 (56, 57, 60) cm. BO loosely.

front

Work same as back until piece measures 16 (17, 17½, 18)"/40.5 (43, 44.5, 45.5) cm.
SHAPE NECK: Work 18 (20, 22, 23) sts. Join a second ball of yarn and BO center 14 sts. Work to end of row. Working both sides at once, BO at each neck edge 3 sts once, then dec 1 st every other row 3 times—12 (14, 16,

17) sts remain for each shoulder. Work even until piece measures same as back. BO loosely.

sleeves

CO 26 (30, 30, 32) sts. Work in St st, and *at the same time* inc 1 st at each end every 6th row 7 (7, 8, 8) times. *(Note: For better seams, work incs 2 sts in from edges.)* Work even until piece measures 16 (16.5, 16.5, 17)"/40.5 (42, 42, 43) cm.
SHAPE CAP: BO 3 sts at beg of next 2 rows. Then dec 1 st at each edge every other row 10 (11, 12, 12) times. Then BO 2 sts at beginning of next 4 rows. BO remaining 6 (8, 8, 10) sts.

finishing

Sew shoulder seams. Sew on sleeves. Sew side and sleeve seams. (See page 15 for details on sewing seams.)
No finishing on neck is required. If desired, a single crochet will finish it nicely (see page 16).

DESIGNER'S NOTES

This is the same pattern as Kenya, except that it uses a stitch pattern that is a multiple of four plus one. So you'll need to delete or add one stitch to compensate for this specific rib. If you wanted to do the entire sweater in the mock rib, you would also have to change the beginning stitch number for the sleeves. For example, 25 (29, 29, 33) would be the number of stitches you cast on for a ribbed sleeve.

If you like, you can also use the neck shaping of Eve and make the mock turtleneck in rib pattern. Just make sure to pick up a multiple of four plus one. Picking up 73 or 77 stitches would work for this pattern in this gauge.

When increasing in this rib or any complicated pattern, sometimes it is very hard to work your increases in two stitches from the edges. I choose to increase on the very edge stitch when I am working in pattern. It is also helpful to use a stitch marker one pattern repeat in from each edge. That way what's between the markers stays consistent, and you can see the pattern clearly. Outside the markers, where you are increasing (and where it is very hard to see the pattern), you can count backward from your marker to determine where you are in the pattern.

Ruby

Ruby is a sexier variation of Kenya that starts with a mock rib pattern ending above the bust, where a second yarn is added to create a contrasting yoke and sleeves in a different stitch pattern. Together, they give the sweater a delightful dirndl effect.

INSTRUCTIONS

rib pattern:

* K3, P1 * repeat end K1

back

With size 10 needles and MC, CO 65 (69, 73, 77) sts. Work even in rib pattern until piece measures 13 (14, 14, 15)"/33 (35.5, 35.5, 38) cm. Change to CC and rev St st (some of you who are more modest might not wish to start the CC until 2 or 3 inches/5 or 7.5 cm after arm-hole shaping). *At the same time:*

SHAPE ARMHOLE: BO 3 sts at beg of next 2 rows, then dec 1 st at each edge every other row 4 (5, 5, 6) times—51 (53, 57, 59) sts. Work even until piece measures 20 (22, 22, 24)"/51 (56, 56, 61) cm. BO loosely.

front

Work same as back until piece measures 17 (18, 18, 19)"/43 (45.5, 45.5, 48.5) cm.
SHAPE NECK: Work 18 (20, 22, 23) sts, join a second ball of yarn and BO center 15 sts, work to end of row. Working both sides at once, BO

at each neck edge 3 sts once, then dec 1 st every other row 3 times—12 (14, 16, 17) sts remaining for each shoulder. Work even until piece measures same as back. BO loosely.

sleeves

With size 10 needles and MC, CO 25 (29, 29, 33) sts. Work in St st, and *at the same time,* inc 1 st at each end every 6th row 7 (7, 8, 8) times. *(Note: For better seams, work incs 2 sts in from edges.)* Work even until piece measures 16 (16½, 16½, 17)"/40.5 (42, 42, 43) cm.
SHAPE CAP: BO 3 sts at beg of next 2 rows. Then dec 1 st at each edge every other row 10 (11, 12, 12) times. Then BO 2 sts at beginning of next 4 rows. BO remaining 5 (7, 7, 11) sts loosely.

finishing

Sew shoulder seams. Sew on sleeves. Sew side and sleeve seams. (See page 15 for details on sewing seams.)
No finishing on neck is required. If desired, a single crochet (see page 16) will finish it nicely.

Skill level | EASY

Sizes

SMALL (Medium, Large, Extra-Large)
Instructions are given for smallest size, with larger sizes in parentheses. When only one number is given, it applies to all sizes.

Finished measurements

CHEST 37 (40, 42, 45)"/94 (101.5, 106.5, 114) cm
LENGTH 20½ (22, 22½, 24)"/52 (56, 57, 61) cm

Materials

MC: 5 (6, 6, 7) skeins Jade Sapphire Maju (100% silk: 1¾ oz/50 g; 85 yds/76 m) in #11A Red
CC: 3 (4, 4, 5) skeins Trendsetter Flora (76% viscose, 24% poly: ¾ oz/25 g; 75 yds/66 m) in #720 Red

Needles

Size 10 (6 mm) or size needed to obtain gauge
Size H-8 (5 mm) crochet hook (optional)

Gauge

14 sts and 18 rows = 4"/10 cm over St st
To save time, take time to check gauge.

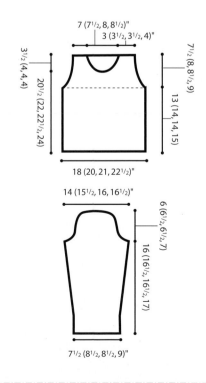

7 (7½, 8, 8½)"
3 (3½, 3½, 4)"
3½ (4, 4, 4)"
20½ (22, 22½, 24)"
7½ (8, 8½, 9)"
13 (14, 14, 15)"
18 (20, 21, 22½)"

14 (15½, 16, 16½)"
6 (6½, 6½, 7)"
16 (16½, 16½, 17)"
7½ (8½, 8½, 9)"

knitted broomstick lace

These three sweaters, although of different styles, have one thing in common: The tank, the long-sleeve sweater, and the sleeveless shell were all knitted using the same intricate-looking stitch pattern, which forms rows of lacy squares resembling broomstick-lace crochet.

This beautiful tank is knitted with a softly variegated cotton-blend yarn in a stitch pattern that knits up quickly and is fun to do. Wear it with any one of different accent-colored tanks underneath to create several looks with a single garment.

Goldi

DESIGNER'S NOTES

By using size 13 needles and wrapping the yarn around your needle twice, you end up with a texture that closely resembles broomstick lace. Don't be intimidated by row 2. There are very clear step-by-step instructions that have been tested by a novice knitter. You can do it!

In addition to the fact that this is a beautiful garment, it is also fast to make. The four-row repeat is 1¼ inches/3 cm. Think about it, knitters: twelve repeats, and you're at the armhole!

INSTRUCTIONS

pattern

Row 1: With size 13 needles, k1,* knit wrapping twice around needle.* Rep end k1.
Row 2: With size 9 needles, p1, then slip next four stitches onto right-hand needle, dropping all wraps to make long stitches. Put back on left-hand needle and knit into all four loops as if they were one stitch. Do not take off needle. Bring yarn to the front and purl into that same stitch. (Do not take off needle.) Bring yarn around to back. K1. (Do not take off needle.) Bring yarn to the front and purl into that same stitch. THEN TAKE OFF LEFT-HAND NEEDLE. End p1.
Rows 3 and 4: With size 9 needles, knit.
Repeat rows 1–4 for pattern.

back

With size 9 needles, CO 54 (58, 62, 66) sts.
Work in pattern stitch until piece measures 13

(14, 14, 15)"/33 (35.5, 35.5, 38) cm.
SHAPE ARMHOLE: BO 4 sts at beg of next 2 rows. Work even until piece measures 20½ (22, 22½, 23)"/52 (56, 57, 58.5) CM. BO loosely.

front

Work same as back until piece measures 17 (18, 18½, 19)"/43 (45.5, 47, 48.5) cm.
SHAPE NECK: Work 10 (10, 14, 14) sts, join a second ball of yarn, and BO center 26 (30, 26, 30) sts; work to end of row. Working both sides at once, work even until piece measures same as back. BO loosely.

finishing

Sew shoulder seams and side seams (see page 15).

Skill level | INTERMEDIATE

Sizes

SMALL (Medium, Large, Extra-Large)
Instructions are given for smallest size, with larger sizes in parentheses. When only one number is given, it applies to all sizes.

Finished measurements

CHEST 36 (39, 41, 44)"/91 (99, 104, 112) cm
LENGTH 20½ (22, 22½, 23)"/52 (56, 57, 58.5) cm

Materials

2 (3, 3, 3) skeins Colinette Giotto (50% cotton, 40% rayon, 10% nylon; 3½ oz/100 g; 156 yds/141 m) in #76 Lichen

Needles

Size 9 (5.5 mm) and size 13 (8 mm) needles or size needed to obtain gauge (*Note: The size 13 needles must be straight.*)

Gauge

12 sts and 12 rows = 4"/10 cm over St st
To save time, take time to check gauge.

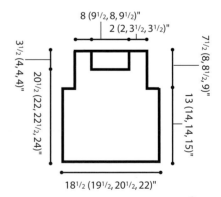

Whatever the weather, this everywhere sweater will see you through: It's Goldi with sleeves. It looks great with jeans for Sunday brunch or over a glitter tank top for an evening out. If the temperature falls, wear the sweater over a black cashmere turtleneck.

Goldilocks

Skill level | INTERMEDIATE

sizes

SMALL (Medium, Large, Extra-Large)
Instructions are given for smallest size, with
larger sizes in parentheses. When only one
number is given, it applies to all sizes.

Finished measurements

CHEST 36 (39, 41, 44)"/91 (99, 104, 112) cm
LENGTH 20½ (22, 22½, 23)"/52 (56, 57, 58.5) cm

Materials

4 (5, 5, 5) skeins Colinette Giotto (50% cotton,
40% rayon, 10% nylon: 3½oz/100 g; 156
yds/141 m) in #76 Lichen

Needles

Size 9 (5.5 mm) and size 13 (8 mm) or size
needed to obtain gauge

Gauge

12 sts and 12 rows = 4"/10 cm over St st
To save time, take time to check gauge.

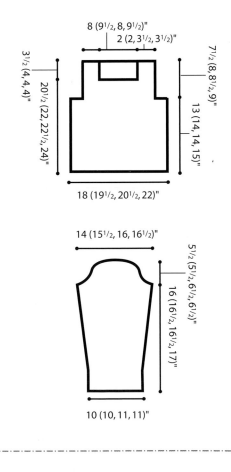

INSTRUCTIONS

pattern

Row 1: With size 13 needles, k1,* knit wrapping twice around needle.* Rep end k1.
Row 2: With size 9 needles, p1, then slip next four stitches onto right-hand needle, dropping all wraps to make long stitches. Put back on left-hand needle and knit into all four loops as if they were one stitch. Do not take off needle. Bring yarn to the front and purl into that same stitch. (Do not take off needle.) Bring yarn around to back. K1. (Do not take off needle.) Bring yarn to the front and purl into that same stitch. THEN TAKE OFF LEFT-HAND NEEDLE. End p1.
Rows 3 and 4: With size 9 needles, knit.
Repeat rows 1–4 for pattern.

back

With size 9 needles, CO 54 (58, 62, 66) sts.
Work in pattern stitch until piece measures 13 (14, 14, 15)"/33 (35.5, 35.5, 38) cm.
SHAPE ARMHOLE: BO 4 (4, 4, 4) sts at beg of next 2 rows. Work even until piece measures 20½ (22, 22½, 23)"/52 (56, 57, 58.5) cm. BO loosely.

front

Work same as back until piece measures 17 (18, 18½, 19)"/43 (45.5, 47, 48.5) cm.

SHAPE NECK: Work 10 (10, 14, 14) sts, join a second ball of yarn, and BO center 26 (30, 26, 30) sts; work to end of row. Working both sides at once, work even until piece measures same as back. BO loosely.

sleeves

With size 9 needles, CO 30 (30, 34, 34) sts. Work in pattern as for back. *At the same time,* increase one stitch at each end every 4th row, 8 times, until piece measures 16 (16½, 16½, 17)"/40.5 (42, 42, 43) cm. (For details on step-by-step increases for this specific pattern, follow instructions below. For those of you who are already whiz kids, I'm sure you'll have your own idea of how to incorporate the pattern in your increases and decreases.)
SHAPE CAP: BO 4 sts at beginning of next two rows. Then dec 1 st at each edge, every other row 10 (10, 12, 12) times. BO remaining 12 (12, 12, 12) sts.

finishing

Sew shoulder seams. Sew on sleeves. Sew side and sleeve seams. (See page 15 for details on sewing seams.)
This pattern is a multiple of four stitches, which is why the neck and the armhole have a square shape. Try working with ribbon, which

is my personal choice because it shows off this pattern stitch so well. The ribbon's natural drape and gravity smooth the square into more of a "U" shape. If you choose a crisp or harder yarn, such as a rope or Egyptian cotton, the square shape will be more pronounced. But we can't exactly increase the sleeves by sets of 4 or we'd have a pretty funky-looking sleeve.

In increasing the sleeves for Goldilocks, follow this pattern:

Row 1: With size 13 needles, k1,* knit wrapping twice around needle.* Rep end k1.

Row 2: With size 9 needles, p1, then slip next four stitches onto right-hand needle, dropping all wraps to make long stitches. Put back on left-hand needle and knit into all four loops as if it were one stitch. Do not take off needle. Bring yarn to the front and purl into that same stitch. (Do not take off needle.) Bring yarn around to back. K1. (Do not take off needle.) Bring yarn to the front and purl into that same stitch. THEN TAKE OFF LEFT-HAND NEEDLE. End p1.

Row 3: Knit.

Row 4: K1, inc, k to the last st, inc 1, k1.

Row 5: With size 13 needles, k2,* knit wrapping twice around needle.* Rep end k2.

Row 6: With size 9 needles, p2, then slip next four stitches onto right-hand needle, dropping all wraps to make long stitches. Put back on left-hand needle and knit into all four loops as if they were one stitch. Do not take off needle. Bring yarn to the front and purl into that same stitch. (Do not take off needle.) Bring yarn

around to back. K1. (Do not take off needle.) Bring yarn to the front and purl into that same stitch. THEN TAKE OFF LEFT-HAND NEEDLE. End p2.

Row 7: Knit.

Row 8: K1, inc, k to the last st, inc 1, k1.

Row 9: With size 13 needles, k1,* knit wrapping twice around needle.* Rep end k1.

Row 10: With size 9 needles, p1, then slip the next two sts onto right-hand needle, dropping all wraps to make long stitches. Put back on left-hand needle and knit into these 2 loops as if they were one stitch. Do not take off needle. Bring yarn to the front and purl into that same stitch. THEN TAKE OFF LEFT-HAND NEEDLE. * Then slip next four stitches onto right-hand needle, dropping all wraps to make long stitches. Put back on left-hand needle and knit into all four loops as if they were one stitch. (Do not take off needle.) Bring yarn to the front and purl into that same stitch. (Do not take off needle.) Bring yarn around to back. K1. (Do not take off needle.) Bring yarn to the front and purl into that same stitch. THEN TAKE OFF LEFT-HAND NEEDLE.* Rep from * to the last 3 sts, then slip the next two sts onto right-hand needle, dropping all wraps to make long stitches. Put back on left-hand needle and knit into these 2 loops as if they were one stitch. Do not take off needle. Bring yarn to the front and purl into that same stitch. THEN TAKE OFF LEFT-HAND NEEDLE. End p1.

Row 11: Knit.

Row 12: K1, inc, k to the last st, inc 1, k1.

Row 13: With size 13 needles, k1,* knit wrapping twice around needle.* Rep end k1.

Row 14: With size 9 needles, p1, then slip the next 3 sts onto right-hand needle, dropping all wraps to make long stitches. Put back on left-hand needle and knit into these 3 loops as if they were one stitch. Do not take off needle. Bring yarn to the front and purl into that same stitch. THEN TAKE OFF LEFT-HAND NEEDLE. * Then slip next four stitches onto right-hand needle, dropping all wraps to make long stitches. Put back on left-hand needle and knit into all four loops as if they were one stitch. Do not take off needle. Bring yarn to the front and purl into that same stitch. (Do not take off needle.) Bring yarn around to back. K1. (Do not take off needle.) Bring yarn to the front and purl into that same stitch. THEN TAKE OFF LEFT-HAND NEEDLE*. Rep from * to the last 4 sts, then slip the next two sts onto right-hand needle, dropping all wraps to make long stitches. Put back on left-hand needle and knit into these 3 loops as if they were one stitch. Do not take off needle. Bring yarn to the front and purl into that same stitch. THEN TAKE OFF LEFT-HAND NEEDLE. End p1.

Rep rows 1–12 for sleeve inc pattern.

To make the cap sleeve, use the same method and follow the sleeve pattern for rows 1–12. EXCEPT: Instead of increases, make decreases. BO 4 sts at beginning of the next 2 rows. Then dec 1 st at each end every other row 8 (8, 10, 10) times (remember to dec on the third row). BO rem 18 sts.

See how different you can make Jessica look from Goldi, just by adding a yarn of contrasting color and texture to define the pattern rows? The broomstick-lace pattern in this shell is striking in a very bright multicolored ribbon set off by bands of glittery black yarn.

Jessica

DESIGNER'S NOTES

This stitch pattern offers so many creative ideas. Take combining yarn colors and textures, for example. Putting combinations like a light olive green with a dark olive green would give you a tone-on-tone effect. And wouldn't it be yummy to do Jessica in gold ribbon as the main color and white angora as the contrasting color? Or flip the colors and have the angora as the main color and the gold ribbon as the contrasting color. Same pattern, totally different looks.

This pattern is also beautiful as just a border. If you'd like, do the four-row repeat for 3 inches/7.5 cm and continue in the main color and stockinette stitch. You can follow the same pattern and create a plain sweater with a beautiful accented border. Or knit Goldilocks in stockinette and just do the accent border for the cuffs. Oh, I could just design forever!

INSTRUCTIONS

pattern

Row 1: With size 13 needles and MC, k1,* knit wrapping twice around needle.* Rep end k1.

Row 2: With size 9 needles and MC, p1, then slip next four stitches onto right-hand needle, dropping all wraps to make long stitches. Put back on left-hand needle and knit into all four loops as if they were one stitch. Do not take off needle. Bring yarn to the front and purl into that same stitch. (Do not take off needle.) Bring yarn around to back. k1. (Do not take off needle.) Bring yarn to the front and purl into that same stitch. THEN TAKE OFF LEFT-HAND NEEDLE. End p1.

Rows 3 and 4: With size 9 needles and CC, knit.

Repeat rows 1–4 for pattern.

back and front

With size 9 needles, CO 54 (58, 62, 66) sts. Work in pattern stitch until piece measures 13 (14, 14, 15)"/33 (35.5, 35.5, 38) cm.

SHAPE ARMHOLE: BO 4 (4, 4, 4) sts at beg of next 2 rows. Work even until piece measures 17 (18, 18½, 19)"/43 (45.5, 47, 48.5) cm.

SHAPE NECK: Work 10 (10, 14, 14) sts, join a second ball of yarn, and BO center 26 (30, 26, 30) sts; work to end of row. Working both sides at once, work 10 (10, 14, 14) sts until piece measures 20½ (22, 22½, 23)"/52 (56, 57, 61) cm. BO.

finishing

Sew shoulder seams. Sew on sleeves. Sew side and sleeve seams. (See page 15 for details on sewing seams.)

Skill level | INTERMEDIATE

Sizes

SMALL (Medium, Large, Extra-Large) Instructions are given for smallest size, with larger sizes in parentheses. When only one number is given, it applies to all sizes.

Finished measurements

CHEST 36 (39, 41, 44)"/91 (99, 104, 112) cm
LENGTH 20½ (22, 22½, 23)"/52 (56, 57, 58.5) cm

Materials

MC: 3 (3, 4, 4) skeins Lion Brand Yarn Incredible (100% nylon: 1¾ oz/50 g; 110 yds/100 m) in #207 Purple Party

CC: 2 (2, 2, 3) skeins Lion Brand Yarn Glitterspun (60% acrylic, 27% cupro, 13% polyester: 1¾ oz/50 g; 115 yds/105 m) in #153 Onyx

Needles

Size 9 (5.5 mm) and size 13 (8 mm) or size needed to obtain gauge

Gauge

12 sts and 12 rows = 4"/10 cm over St st
To save time, take time to check gauge.

8 (9½, 8, 9½)"
2 (2, 3½, 3½)"
3½ (4, 4, 4)"
20½ (22, 22½, 24)"
7½ (8, 8½, 9)"
13 (14, 14, 15)"
18 (19½, 20½, 22)"

the v-neck cardigan

Everyone loves a V-neck cardigan. And any one of these would be perfect for you or someone on your gift list. Katherine, refined in its simplicity, is always in style—with or without its ruffled scarf. Tracy, ablaze in rows of color and shimmering threads, begs to be the center of attention. While Paula may seem prim and proper, the rib knit, boldly contrasting borders, and oversized buttons say otherwise.

Sexy and feminine, this luxurious classic V-neck cardigan is so soft that it floats on your shoulders. The delicate picot edging makes it the perfect topper for any outfit, any time. But add the lush tiered ruffle scarf and—voilà!— get ready to set your inner diva free.

Katherine

DESIGNER'S NOTES

This scarf is a separate garment that can be worn in other combinations as well. It can be worn draped to frame the jacket, tied, or wrapped around the neck a few times.

If Scarlet O'Hara had worn knits, she would have loved Katherine-with-Ruffles. The three individual tiers of ruffles are knitted separately, then joined together to form a sumptuous scarf. However, one or two tiers would look fabulous as well.

If you'd like to make a more substantial jacket, use a bulkier yarn that gives you the same gauge. In the bulkier yarn, a scarf might be a bit much. I would just do one ruffle instead.

INSTRUCTIONS

back

With size 9 needles and MC, CO 70 (74, 78, 82) sts. Work in St st for 4 rows. In next row for picot: *K2tog, yo * across row. Continue in St st. When piece measures 2"/5cm, dec 1 st at each end every 10th row 3 times. When piece measures 11 (12, 13, 13)"/28 (30.5, 33, 33) cm, inc 1 st at each end every 6th row 3 times. Work until piece measures 14 (14, 15, 15)"/35.5 (35.5, 38, 38) cm.
SHAPE ARMHOLE: BO 5 (5, 6, 7) sts at beg of next 2 rows, then dec 1 st at each edge every other row 3 (4, 5, 7) times until piece measures 22 (22, 23½, 24)"/56 (56, 59.5, 61) cm. BO loosely.

front

RIGHT SIDE: With size 9 needles, CO 36

(38, 40, 42) sts. Work as for back, working side shaping at side edge only, until piece measures 14 (14, 15, 15)"/35.5 (35.5, 38, 38) cm.
SHAPE ARMHOLE: BO 5 (5, 6, 7) sts at beg of next 2 rows, then dec 1 st at each edge every other row 5 times. *At the same time:*
SHAPE NECK: Dec 1 st (k1, sl 1, k1, psso) every 4th row, 10 (11, 12, 12) times. When piece measures same as back, BO loosely.
LEFT SIDE: Reverse shaping (dec thus: work to last 3 sts, k2tog, k1).

sleeves

With size 9 needles, CO 32 (32, 36, 36) sts. Work in St st for 4 rows. In next row, for picot: *K2tog, yo* rep across row. Continue in St st and *at the same time,* inc 1 st at each end every 6th row 10 (12, 14, 14) times, until piece

Skill level | EASY/MODERATE

Sizes

SMALL (Medium, Large, Extra-Large) Instructions are given for smallest size, with larger sizes in parentheses. When only one number is given, it applies to all sizes.

Finished measurements

CHEST 36 (39, 42, 45)"/91 (99, 106.5, 114) cm
LENGTH 22 (22, 23½, 24)"/56 (56, 59.5, 61) cm

Materials

GARMENT
MC: 10 (12, 13, 15) skeins Rowan Yarns Kid Silk Haze (70% super kid mohair, 30% silk: 1 oz/25 g; 229 yds/210 m) in #581 Meadow
SCARF
CC A: 2 skeins Rowan Yarns Kid Silk Haze in #592 Heavenly
CC B: 1 skein Rowan Yarns Kid Silk Haze in #581 Meadow
CC C: 1 skein C Rowan Yarns Kid Silk Haze in #590 Ivory

Needles

Size 9 (6 mm) and size 8 (5 mm) circular or size needed to obtain gauge

Gauge

14 sts and 18 rows = 4"/10 cm over St st
To save time, take time to check gauge.

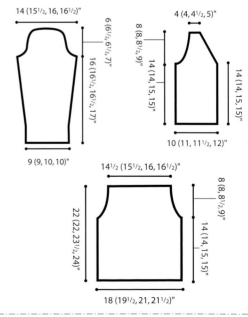

Katherine
(CONTINUED)

measures 15½ (16, 16, 16½)"/39.5 (40.5, 40.5, 42) cm. (*Note: For better seams, make your increases leaving 2 edge stitches on each end.*)
SHAPE CAP: BO 5 (5, 6, 7) sts at beg of next 2 rows. Then dec 1 st at each edge every other row 10 (11, 12, 13) times. Then BO 3 sts at beginning of next 4 rows. BO remaining sts loosely.

finishing

Sew shoulder seams together (see page 15). With circular size 8 needles, pick up right band: Pick up 3 sts,* CO 2 sts and skip 2 rows on garment, pick up 9 (10, 11, 12)* sts repeat from * four more times. Pick up (26, 28, 30,

30) sts up V-neck, 20 (20, 22, 22) sts from back, and 68 (72, 76, 80) sts down left band. Work in St st for 4 rows. In next row for picot: *K2tog, yo* across row. Continue in St st for 4 more rows. BO. Tack in with a loose whip st. Sew sleeves and side seams (see page 15).

ruffled scarf

RUFFLE A: With circular size 8 needles and A, CO 600 sts and work in St st until piece measures 2½"/6.5 cm. K3tog across row—200 sts. Continue St st until piece measures 6½"/16.5 cm. Leave sts on needle.
RUFFLE B: With circular size 8 needles and B, CO 600 sts and work in St st until piece

measures 2½"/6.5 cm. K3tog across row— 200 sts. Continue in St st until piece measures 4½"/12 cm. Leave sts on spare needle.
RUFFLE C: With circular size 8 needles and C, CO 600 sts and work in St st until piece measures 2¼"/5.5 cm. K3tog across row—200 sts. Purl 1 row. Leave sts on needle.
ASSEMBLY OF RUFFLES: With right side facing, layer ruffles as follows: A on bottom, B in the middle, and C on top. With A, holding needles parallel, knit into first st on each needle, working 1 st of A, B, and C tog. Rep across row, joining 3 ruffles into scarf. Purl 1 row. BO all sts loosely. Do not block.

Tracy is Katherine worked in Prism Arts Wild Stuff yarn in the colorway Amber. Yes, this yarn is expensive, but it's worth the experience—and the result! It's a dream to work with and every three rows is a surprise: You get a new texture and color to knit!

Tracy

INSTRUCTIONS

back

With size 10 needles, CO 70 (74, 78, 82) sts. Work in garter st for 1½"/3.8 cm. Then St st until piece measures 15 (16, 17, 17)"/38 (40.5, 43, 43) cm.

SHAPE ARMHOLE: BO 5 (5, 6, 7) sts at beg of next 2 rows, then dec 1 st at each edge every other row 3 (4, 5, 7) times. BO when piece measures 23 (24, 25, 26)"/58.5 (61, 63.5, 66) cm.

front

RIGHT SIDE: With size 10 needles, CO 36 (38, 40, 42) sts. Work in garter st for 1½"/3.8 cm. Then St st until piece measures 11 (12, 13, 13)"/28 (30.5, 33, 33) cm.

SHAPE ARMHOLE: BO 5 (5, 6, 7) sts at beg of next 2 rows, then dec 1 st at each edge every other row 3 (4, 5, 7) times. *At the same time:*

SHAPE NECK: Dec 1 st (k1, sl 1, k1, psso) every 4th row, 10 (11, 12, 12) times. BO when piece measures same as back.

LEFT SIDE: Reverse shaping (dec thus: work to last 3 sts, k2tog, k1).

sleeves

With size 10 needles, CO 30 (32, 34, 36) sts. Work in garter st for 1½"/3.8 cm. Then work in St st, inc 1 st at each end every 6th row 10 (12, 13, 14) times, until piece measures 15½

(16, 16, 16½)"/39.5 (40.5, 40.5, 42) cm. *(Note: For better seams, make your increases leaving 2 edge stitches on each end.)*

SHAPE CAP: BO 5 (5, 6, 7) sts at beg of next 2 rows. Then dec 1 st at each edge every other row 10 (11, 12, 13) times. Then BO 2 sts at beginning of next 6 rows. BO remaining stitches loosely.

finishing

Sew shoulder seams tog (see page 15). With circular size 9 needles, pick up 70 (74, 78, 82) sts up right side, 20 (20, 22, 22, 24) sts across back, 70 (74, 78, 82) sts down left front. Knit 5 rows. Buttonhole row: K 4, *BO 2 sts, knit 16 sts* repeat 2 more times. Knit to end. Next row: Knit to first buttonhole *CO 2 st over the 2 bound off sts, knit 16* repeat 2 more times, end knit 4 sts. BO 46 (48, 50, 52) sts at beg of next 2 rows.

SHAPE SHAWL COLLAR: Dec 1 st at each edge every row, *at the same time,* *K13 (14, 15, 16) place marker * rep from * end k13 (14, 15, 16) sts. Inc 1 st after each marker every 6th row 3 times. Knit 6 more rows. BO loosely. Sew sleeves and side seams (see page 15).

Skill level | EASY

Sizes

SMALL (Medium, Large, Extra-Large) Instructions are given for smallest size, with larger sizes in parentheses. When only one number is given, it applies to all sizes.

Finished measurements

CHEST 37 (40, 42, 45)"/94 (101.5, 106.5, 114) cm
LENGTH 23 (24, 25, 26)"/58.5 (61, 63.5, 66) cm

Materials

3 (3½, 4, 4) skeins Prism Arts Wild Stuff yarn (wool, cotton, mohair, nylon, poly, linen, alpaca: 3½ oz/100 g; 300 yds/270 m) in colorway Amber

Needles

Size 10 (6 mm) and size 9 circular or size needed to obtain gauge

Gauge

14 sts and 18 rows = 4"/10 cm over St st
To save time, take time to check gauge.

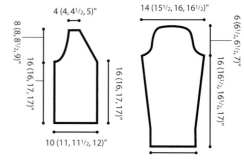

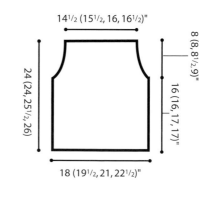

When you want to assert your authority but still show your soft side, this tailored, two-toned, bordered V-neck cardigan is the perfect look. The simple K3, P1 rib stitch used in the body of the cardigan gives nice line and texture, while the black accent borders add sharp definition.

Paula

INSTRUCTIONS

pattern stitch

Row 1: *P3, k1* rep end p3.

Row 2: *K3, p1* rep end k3.

Repeat rows 1 and 2 for pattern.

back

With size 8 needles and MC, CO 83 (87, 91, 95) sts. Work in pattern stitch (above) until piece measures 9 (10, 11, 12)"/23 (25.5, 28, 30.5) cm.

SHAPE ARMHOLE: BO 4 (4, 5, 6) sts at beg of next 2 rows, then dec 1 st at each edge every other row 4 (5, 5, 5) times. When the piece measures 18 (18, 19½, 20)"/45.5 (45.5, 49.5, 51) cm, loosely BO remaining 67 (69, 71, 73) sts.

front

RIGHT SIDE: With size 8 needles and MC, CO 39 (43, 47, 51) sts. Work as for back until piece measures 8 (9, 10, 11)"/20.5 (23, 25.5, 28) cm.

SHAPE NECK: Dec 1 st (k1, sl 1, k1, psso) every 6th row 13 (14, 15, 15) times until piece measures 10 (10, 11,12)"/25.5 (25.5, 28, 30.5) cm.

SHAPE ARMHOLE: BO 4 (4, 5, 6) sts at beg of next 2 rows, then dec 1 st at each edge every other row 4 (5, 5, 6) times. When piece measures same as back, loosely BO remaining 18 (20, 22, 25) sts.

LEFT SIDE: Reverse shaping (dec thus: work to last 3 sts, k2tog, k1).

sleeves

With size 8 needles and MC, CO 39 (43, 43, 47) sts. Work in rib pattern as for back, *at the same time*, inc 1 st at each end every 4th row 13 (13, 14, 14) times, until piece measures 12 (13, 13, 13)"/30.5 (33, 33, 33) cm.

SHAPE CAP: BO 4 (4, 5, 6) sts at beg of next 2 rows. Then dec 1 st at each edge every other row 4 (5, 6, 7) times. Then BO 2 (3, 3, 3) sts at beginning of next 4 rows. BO remaining 28 (26, 23, 23) sts loosely.

finishing

Sew shoulder seams, sleeves, and side seams together (see page 15). With size 7 needles and CC, make bottom band: CO 142 (148, 154, 160) sts, and work in St st for 5"/12.5 cm. BO loosely. Let the roll happen and sew bottom border to body. With size 7 needles and CC, CO 40 (44, 48, 48) sts work in St st for 5"/12.5 cm. BO. Let the roll happen and sew bottom border to sleeves. Sew sleeves.

neck, body, and sleeveband

Neckband: with size 7 needles and CC, make button band: CO 200 (208, 216, 224) sts. Work in St st for 2½"/6.5 cm with right side facing. Knit 8, BO 4 sts, knit 16 sts, BO 4 sts knit to the end. Purl to first BO and CO 4 sts, purl to second BO and CO 4 sts. Continue in St st for another 2½"/6.5 cm. BO loosely. Body band: With size 7 (4.5 mm) needles and CC, CO 150 (160, 170, 180) sts. Work in St st for 5 inches (12.5 cm). BO loosely. Sleeve band: With size 7 (4.5 mm) needles and CC, CO 40 (42, 46, 48) sts. Work in St st for 5 inches (12.5 cm). BO loosely. Let the roll happen and sew onto body leaving a good inch/2.5 cm of roll on the outside of garment. Sew buttons.

Skill level | INTERMEDIATE

Sizes

SMALL (Medium, Large, Extra-Large) Instructions are given for smallest size, with larger sizes in parentheses. When only one number is given, it applies to all sizes.

Finished measurements

CHEST 38 (40, 43, 45)"/91 (99, 106.5, 114) cm

LENGTH 22 (22, 23½, 24)"/56 (56, 59.5, 61) cm

Materials

MC: 13 (14, 15, 16) skeins GGH Velour (100% polyamid: 7/8 oz/25 g; 64 yds/58 m) in #8 Olive

CC: 4 (5, 5, 5) skeins GGH Velour in #17 Black

2 1½-inch/3.8-cm buttons

Needles

Size 8 (5 mm) and size 7 (4.5 mm) or size needed to obtain gauge

Gauge

17 sts and 22 rows = 4"/10 cm over St st

To save time, take time to check gauge.

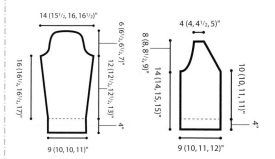

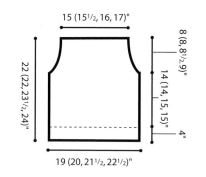

the side-to-side kimono

Centuries old, the kimono is still the ultimate wrap for style and comfort. As a jacket—worn belted or not—the loose sleeves and crossover front endow it with a roomy but not shapeless fit. The three distinct styles in this sweater group will make you feel like a graceful geisha whether you're at the office, out for a dress-up evening, or lounging around the house.

Suki

Roomy and refined, this stunning kimono jacket turns a daytime tank top into an evening ensemble. Done in Prism "eyelash" yarns, it is knit from sleeve to sleeve, forming slimming vertical stripes. Adding the obi-sash belt lends the garment stylish Japanese flair.

INSTRUCTIONS

Starting at the sleeve: With size 8 needles and CC A, CO 70 (72, 74, 76) sts. Work in St st for 14 rows. Tie on CC B, purl 2 rows. Then, continue in St st for 13 more rows. Tie on MC and work in St st until piece measures 13 (13, 14, 14)"/33 (33, 35.5, 35.5) cm from start of MC. Then inc 1 st at each edge every other row 4 times. Then CO for body 44 (48, 52, 56) sts at the beg of next 2 rows. Place stitch marker—166 (176, 186, 196) sts. Continue until piece measures 4½ (4½, 5, 5½)"/12 (12, 12.5, 14) cm from marker. Divide in half, work 83 (88, 93, 98) sts, then put remaining 83 (88, 93, 98) stitches onto a stitch holder. Working the back only, continue in St st until piece measures 17 (19, 21, 22)"/43 (48.5, 53.5, 56) cm from marker. Put on a holder and return to front 83 (88, 93, 98) sts. BO 2 sts at beg of neck edge 23 (25, 27, 29) times. Then with CC B, knit 1 row, tie on CC A work St st for 4 rows. BO remaining 37 (38, 39, 40) sts loosely.

LEFT FRONT: With size 8 needles and CC A, CO 37 (38, 39, 40) sts. Work in St st for 4 rows, then tie on CC B and purl 1 row on right side for fold. Tie on MC and work in St st.

SHAPE NECK: CO 2 stitches at neck edge 23 (25, 27, 29) times, for 83 (88, 93, 98) sts.

JOIN: Knit 83 (88, 93, 98) sts of front to the 83 (88, 93, 98) sts of the back. Continue in St st for

4 (4½, 5, 5½)"/10 (12, 12.5, 14) cm. Very loosely BO 44 (48, 52, 56) sts at the beginning of the next 2 rows. Decrease 1 st at each edge every other row 4 times 70 (72, 74, 76) sts. Work in St st until piece measures 13 (13, 14, 14)"/33 (33, 35.5, 35.5) cm. Tie on CC B. Work in St st for 14 rows, tie on A, purl 1, St st for 13 rows. BO loosely.

finishing: sew side seams together (see page 15).

COLLAR: With size 8 needles and CC B, pick up 50 (54, 58, 62) sts up right front, 36 (38, 40, 42) sts from back, and 50 (54, 58, 62) sts down left front. Work in St st for 14 rows, tie on CC A, purl 1 row, and work in St st for 13 rows. BO loosely. Crochet button loop with size G-6 crochet hook chain 1½"/3.8 cm, leaving 6-inch/15-cm ties to use to attach to garment. Place and sew and sew on button.
BELT: With size 8 needles and CC A, CO 13 sts, tie on CC B and CO 13 more sts. Work in garter st for 24"/61 cm. BO using chain stitch and MC. Embellish as desired. thread through the belt ribbons for tie closure. Using a blunt-ended needle, thread belt ribbon through the middle fronts of the obi-sash, leaving foot-long/30.5-cm-long tails for tying.

Skill level — EASY/MODERATE

Sizes
SMALL (Medium, Large, Extra-Large) Instructions are given for smallest size, with larger sizes in parentheses. When only one number is given, it applies to all sizes.

Finished measurements
CHEST 36 (39, 42, 45)"/91 (99, 106.5, 114) cm
LENGTH 20½ (22, 22½, 24)"/52 (56, 57, 61) cm

Materials
MC: 3 (3½, 4, 4) skeins Prism Arts Cool Stuff (cotton, nylon, poly, linen: 300 yds/270 m) in Tumbleweed
CC A: 2 skeins Prism Arts Bon Bon (100% rayon: 2 oz/56 g; 85 yds/73 m) in #310 Sage
CC B: 2 skeins Prism Arts Bon Bon (100% rayon: 2 oz/56 g; 85 yds/73 m) in #309 Soft Plum
2 yds of 1-inch/2.5-cm silk ribbon
1 1¼-inch/3-cm button
1 large stitch holder
2 markers

Needles
Size 8 (5 mm) or size needed to obtain gauge
Size G-6 crochet hook

Gauge
16 sts and 20 rows = 4"/10 cm over St st
To save time, take time to check gauge.

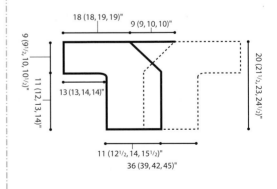

Sara

Could this kimono be any more feminine? With silk ribbons woven through the lacy pattern of its textured rayon stitches, and finished with lots of dainty bows, this vibrant, cuddly kimono will see you through a night with your beloved from the ballroom to the bedroom.

Skill level | Easy/Intermediate

Sizes

SMALL (Medium, Large, Extra-Large) Instructions are given for smallest size, with larger sizes in parentheses. When only one number is given, it applies to all sizes.

Finished measurements

CHEST 36 (39, 42, 45)"/91 (99, 106.5, 114) cm
LENGTH 22 (23½, 25, 26½)"/56 (59.5, 63.5, 67) cm

Materials

12 (13, 14, 16) skeins Plymouth Yarn Company Electra (100% nylon: 1¾ oz/50 g; 125 yds/113 m) in #13 Rosebud
8 yds/8 m of 1-inch/2.5-cm silk ribbon
1 large stitch holder
2 stitch markers

Needles

Size 8 (5 mm) or size needed to obtain gauge

Gauge

16 sts and 20 rows= 4"/10 cm over St st
To save time, take time to check gauge.

INSTRUCTIONS

Starting at the sleeve: With size 8 needles and two strands of yarn, CO 70 (72, 74, 76) sts. Work in St st until Piece measures 7"/18 cm, ending with wrong-side row. Row 1: K1, *yo, k2tog* rep from *. Row 2: Purl. Repeat this yarn-over pattern every 7 (7, 8, 8½)"/18 (18, 20.5, 21.5) cm throughout garment. Continue in St st until piece measures 13 (13, 14, 14)"/33 (33, 35.5, 35.5) cm. Then inc 1 st at each edge every other row 4 times. Then CO 44 (48, 52, 56) sts for body at the beg of next 2 rows. Place marker at end of 2nd row—166 (176, 186, 196) sts. Continue until piece measures 4½ (4½, 5, 5½)"/12 (12.5, 14) cm from marker. Divide in half, work 83 (88, 93, 98) sts, then put remaining 83 (88, 93, 98) stitches onto a holder. Working the back only, continue in St st until piece measures 13½ (13½, 15, 15)"/34 (34, 38, 38) cm from marker. Put on a holder and return to front 83 (88, 93, 98) sts. BO 2 sts at beg of neck edge 23 (25, 27, 29) times. BO remaining 37 (38, 39, 40) sts loosely.

left front

With size 8 needles and two strands of yarn, CO 37 (38, 39, 40) sts. Work in St st.
SHAPE NECK: CO 2 stitches at neck edge 23 (25, 27, 29) times—83 (88, 93, 98) sts.
JOIN: Knit 83 (88, 93, 98) sts of front to the 83 (88, 93, 98) sts of the back. Continue in St st for 4 (4½, 5, 5½)"/10 (12, 12.5, 14) cm. Very loosely BO 44 (48, 52, 56) sts at the beginning of the next 2 rows. Decrease 1 st at each edge every other row 4 times—70 (72, 74, 76) sts. Work in St st until piece measures 13 (13, 14, 14)"/33 (33, 35.5, 35.5) cm. BO loosely.

finishing

Sew side seams together (see page 15). I wove hand-dyed silk ribbon through the eyelet lace pattern, and trimmed it with bows. Then whipstitch the ribbon about 2"/5 cm apart around front, neck bands, and armbands.

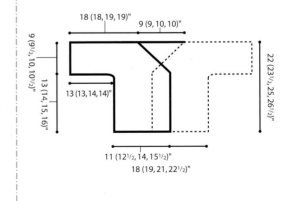

Take Suki, shorten the sleeves, lengthen it to cover your tush as much as you'd like, and you have this velvety-soft, personalized kimono, the perfect cover-up when stepping out of the shower or onto the beach.

Sandy

DESIGNER'S NOTES

The length of this kimono is entirely up to you. If you prefer it short, cast on fewer stitches than suggested. If you need to cover those saddlebags, cast on more to make it longer.

INSTRUCTIONS

Starting at the sleeve: With size 7 needles and CC A, CO 70 (72, 74, 76) sts and knit 2 rows. Tie on MC, St st for 4 rows. Tie on CC B, knit 2 rows. St st 2 rows MC. Tie on CC C, knit 2 rows. Working in St st, repeat color stripes every 5 (5½, 6, 6½)"/12.5 (14, 15, 16.5) cm. *At the same time* as working the color sequence, start armhole shaping until piece measures 4"/10 cm. Then inc 1 st at each edge every other row 4 times. Then CO for body 80 sts at the beg of next 2 rows—238 (240, 242, 244) sts. Place stitch marker. Continue until piece measures 4½ (4½, 5, 5½)"/12 (12, 12.5, 14) cm from marker. Divide in half, work 119 (120, 121, 122) sts, then put remaining stitches onto a holder. Working the back 119 (120, 121, 122) sts only, continue in St st until piece measures 13½ (13½, 15, 15)"/34 (34, 38, 38) cm from marker. Put on a holder and return to front—119 (120, 121, 122) sts. BO 2 sts at beg of neck edge 24 times. Loosely BO remaining 71 (72, 73, 74) sts.

left front

With size 7 needles and CC C, CO 71 (72, 73, 74) sts.

Work in St st, reversing the color stripes.

SHAPE NECK: CO 2 stitches at neck edge 24 times.

JOIN: Knit 119 (120, 121, 122) sts of front to the 119 (120, 121, 122) sts of the back. Continue in St st for 4 (4½, 5, 5½)"/10 (12, 12.5, 14) cm. Very loosely BO 80 sts at the beginning of the next two rows. Decrease 1 st at each edge every other row 4 times—70 (72, 74, 76) sts. Work in St st until piece measures 2"/5 cm. BO.

finishing

Sew side seams together (see page 15). With MC and G-6 crochet hook, chain 1½ inches/3.8 cm, leaving 6"/15 cm to sew belt loop to waist of robe. Make 2.

belt

With size 7 needles and CC C, CO 8 sts. Knit 1 row, change to MC, and work in St st for 54"/137 cm. Change to CC C, knit 1 row. BO.

Skill level | EASY/INTERMEDIATE

Sizes

SMALL (Medium, Large, Extra-Large) Instructions are given for smallest size, with larger sizes in parentheses. When only one number is given, it applies to all sizes.

Finished measurements

CHEST 36 (39, 42, 45)"/91 (99, 106.5, 114) cm
LENGTH 29 (30, 31, 32)"/74 (76, 79, 81) cm

Materials

MC: 9 (10, 11, 12) skeins Crystal Palace Yarns Chenille (100% cotton: 1¾ oz/50 g; 98 yds/89 m) in #1028 White
CC A: 1 skein Crystal Palace Yarns Chenille in #8211 Pink
CC B: 1 skein Crystal Palace Yarns Chenille in #2230 Tangerine
CC C: 1 skein Crystal Palace Yarns Chenille in #2342 Lime
2 stitch markers

Needles

Size 7 (4.5 mm) or size needed to obtain gauge
Size G-6 crochet hook

Gauge

16 sts and 20 rows = 4"/10 cm over St st
To save time, take time to check gauge.

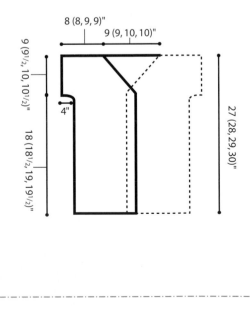

chevron play

In the world of the military, the chevron motif that appears
on the sleeves of officers denotes rank, and it demands a salute.
In the world of fashion, you'll receive plenty of salutes when
you step out in Madonna, the chevron-patterned lace-up halter
top; Sheila, the timeless tank; or Elizabeth, the dazzling
jacket evocative of a butterfly's wings.

Remember the pointy bras Madonna wore when she was touring in the early 1990s? Well, they were the inspiration for this fabulous bustier-style halter top. Eleven heathery colors, separated by black, form the chevron design of this body-hugging sweater. Black also laces together the center and side seams.

Madonna

DESIGNER'S NOTES

The whole time I was knitting this, I kept wishing I could see it on Madonna. I knitted pads to go as an interfacing in the bra. Most of you will need to make only one pair. The more flat-chested may need to make two or three.

I would love to see this garment done in just black and gold for evening. The body chevrons could be gold with black stripes and the bust could be solid black with gold accents. I wish I had the time to knit that and a skirt to match.

INSTRUCTIONS

stripe pattern

Rows 1 and 2: With CC, knit.
Rows 3, 5, and 7: With #40 k2, yo, k to last 2 sts; yo, K2.
Rows 4, 6, and 8: With #40 purl.
Repeat rows 1–8 with CC and in colors #38, #34, #29, #32, #23, #48, #9, and #7.
Repeat, if necessary, to get adequate length; end with row 2. BO.

chevron pattern

Rows 1 and 2: Knit.
Rows 3, 5, and 7: K2, yo, k15 (17, 19, 21), k2tog in back, k2, k2tog, k15 (17, 19, 21), yo, k2.
Rows 4, 6, and 8: Purl.
Repeat rows 1–8 with CC and in #40, #38, #34, #29, #32, #23, #48, #9, and #7.
Repeat, if necessary, to get adequate length; end with row 2. BO loosely.

back

With size 8 needles and CC, CO 60 (66, 72, 78) sts. Work in stripe pattern until piece measures 11 (12, 13, 14)"/28 (30.5, 33, 35.5) cm. BO loosely.

right front

With size 8 needles and CC, CO 40 (44, 48, 52) sts. Work stripe pattern and chevron pattern.

left front

Same as right front.

bust

With size 8 needles and CC, CO 40 (42, 44, 46) sts. Working 6 stripes of colors #42 and #20:
Row 1: K17 (18, 19, 20) sts, k2tog in back, k2, k2tog, k17 (18, 19, 20) sts.
Row 2 and all even rows: Knit.

Skill level
INTERMEDIATE/ADVANCED

Sizes
SMALL (Medium, Large, Extra-Large)
Instructions are given for smallest size, with larger sizes in parentheses. When only one number is given, it applies to all sizes.

Finished measurements
CHEST 18 (19½, 21, 22½)"/45.5 (49.5, 53.5, 57) cm
LENGTH 11 (12, 13, 14)"/28 (30.5, 33, 35.5) cm

Materials
MC: Tahki Stacy Charles S. Charles Collection Venus (95% viscose, 5% polyamide: 1¾ oz/50 g; 83 yds/75 m) in following colors: for body, 1 skein each in #40, #38, #34, #29, #32, #23, #48, #9, and #7; for bust, 1 skein each in #42 and #20
CC: 1 (1, 1, 2) skein Tahki Stacy Charles Cotton Classic (100% cotton: 1¾ oz/50 g; 108 yds/98 m) in #3002 Black

Needles
Size 8 (5 mm) or size needed to obtain gauge

Gauge
16 sts and 20 rows = 4"/10 cm over St st
To save time, take time to check gauge.

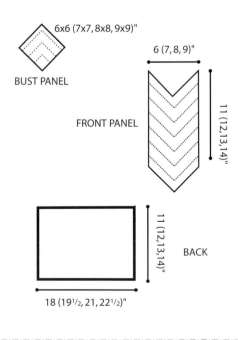

6x6 (7x7, 8x8, 9x9)"

BUST PANEL

6 (7, 8, 9)"

FRONT PANEL

11 (12, 13, 14)"

11 (12, 13, 14)"

BACK

18 (19½, 21, 22½)"

Madonna
(CONTINUED)

Row 3: K16 (17, 18, 19) sts, k2tog in back, k2, k2tog, k16 (17, 18, 19) sts.

Row 5: K15 (16, 17, 18) sts, k2tog in back, k2, k2tog, k15 (16, 17, 18) sts.

Row 7: K14 (15, 16, 17) sts ... etc.

Row 9: K13 (14, 15, 16) sts ... etc. Continue decreasing in this manner until one stitch remains. BO last stitch.

finishing

NECK BAND: With size 8 needles and right side facing, start at bottom of right front. Pick up 20 (22, 24, 26) sts from outer edge of bust. Then CO 70 more stitches for strap. Work in garter st 2 rows CC, 2 rows #29 twice, end 2 rows CC. BO very loosely.

JOINING: With CC, (or a silk ribbon or shoelace), triple weave center and side seams together through yarn overs as you would lace up a shoe.

PADDED INTERFACING: With size 8 needles and CC, triple CO 9 sts and garter st. Dec 1 st at beg of every row until 1 st remains. BO. Make 2 or make 10 and be Dolly Parton!

For those of you who don't favor the braless look of the Madonna halter top, here's the same pattern in the same yarn, but in just one color, with a solid back and wide shoulder straps. Still sexy, but much more sophisticated.

Sheila

INSTRUCTIONS

Use size 8 (5mm) needles throughout.

stripe pattern

Rows 1 and 2: Knit.

Rows 3, 5, and 7: K2, yo, k to last 2 sts yo, k2.

Rows 4, 6, and 8: Purl.

Row 9: Purl.

Row 10: Knit.

Repeat rows 3–10 for pattern. Work until piece measures 11 (12, 13, 14)"/28 (30.5, 33, 35.5) cm.

chevron pattern

Rows 1 and 2: Knit.

Rows 3, 5, and 7: K2, yo, k15 (17, 19, 21), k2tog in back, k2, k2tog, k15 (17, 19 21), yo, k2.

Rows 4, 6, and 8: Purl.

Row 9: Purl.

Row 10: Knit.

Repeat rows 3–10 for pattern. Work until piece measures 11 (12, 13, 14)"/28 (30.5, 33, 35.5) cm.

back

CO 60 (66, 72, 78) sts. Work in stripe pattern until piece measures 12 (13, 14, 15)"/30.5 (33, 35.5, 38) cm. BO loosely.

SHAPE ARMHOLE: BO 5 stitches at the beginning of next 2 rows. Then, decrease 1 st at each edge every other row 4 (5, 6, 7) times. Work even until piece measures 18½ (20,

21½, 23)"/47 (51, 55, 58.5) cm. BO loosely.

front

RIGHT SIDE: CO 40 (44, 48, 52) sts. Work chevron pattern.

LEFT SIDE: Same as right side.

bust

CO 40 (42, 44, 46) sts.

Row 1: K17 (18, 19, 20) sts, k2tog in back, K2, k2tog, k17 (18, 19, 20) sts.

Row 2 and all even rows: Knit.

Row 3: K16 (17, 18, 19) sts, k2tog in back, k2, k2tog, k16 (17, 18, 19) sts.

Row 5: K15 (16, 17, 18) sts, k2tog in back, k2, k2tog, k15 (16, 17, 18) sts.

Row 7: K14 (15, 16, 17) sts . . . etc.

Row 9: K13 (14, 15, 16) sts . . . etc. Continue decreasing in this manner until one stitch remains. BO last stitch.

finishing

SHOULDER STRAPS: With right side facing, start at bottom of right front at the side seam. Pick up 20 (22, 24, 26) sts from outer edge of bust. Then CO 20 (22, 24, 16) sts for strap. Work in garter st for 2"/5 cm. BO very loosely.

Sew shoulders, center, and side seams together (see page 15).

Skill level | INTERMEDIATE

Sizes

SMALL (Medium, Large, Extra-Large) Instructions are given for smallest size, with larger sizes in parentheses. When only one number is given, it applies to all sizes.

Finished measurements

CHEST 18 (19½, 21, 22½)"/45.5 (49.5, 53.5, 57) cm

LENGTH 18½ (20, 21½, 23)"/47 (51, 55, 58.5) cm

Materials

5 (6, 7, 8) skeins Tahki Stacy Charles S. Charles Collection Venus (95% viscose, 5% polamide: 1¾ oz/50 g; 83 yds/75 m) in #38

Needles

Size 8 (5 mm) or size needed to obtain gauge

Gauge

16 sts and 20 rows = 4"/10 cm over St st
To save time, take time to check gauge.

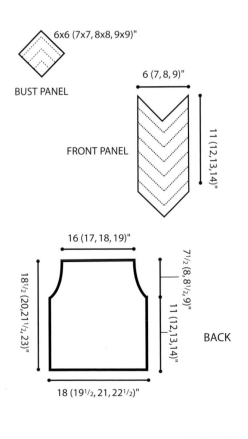

6x6 (7x7, 8x8, 9x9)"

BUST PANEL

6 (7, 8, 9)"

FRONT PANEL

11 (12,13,14)"

16 (17, 18, 19)"

18½ (20,21½, 23)"

7½ (8, 8½, 9)"

11 (12,13,14)"

BACK

18 (19½, 21, 22½)"

Here is the same stunning chevron pattern as Madonna, done as an elegant jacket. The longer length, tapered-to-a-point sleeves, and three-panel back result in a sweater that's sheer drama. Just the thing Elizabeth Taylor would wear to one of her many charity events.

Elizabeth

DESIGNER'S NOTES

This piece will challenge the knitter. It's like a geometric puzzle you put together. For an extraordinary ensemble, try it calf length in a rich burgundy with black velour accents, and wear it with a black silk camisole and wide-legged pants.

INSTRUCTIONS

stripe pattern (colors)

Rows 1 and 2: With CC, knit.
Rows 3, 5, and 7: With E, knit.
Rows 4, 6, and 8: With E, purl.
Repeat rows 1–8 once more (for longer versions, you could repeat each color three or even four times). Change to D, repeat rows 1–8 twice; change to C, repeat rows 1–8 twice; change to B, repeat rows 1–8 twice, change to A repeat rows 1–8 twice; end with Row 2. BO very loosely.

chevron pattern

Rows 1 and 2: Knit.
Rows 3, 5, and 7: K2, M1, k15 (17, 19, 21), k2tog in back, k1, k2tog, k15 (17, 19 21), M1, k2.
Rows 4, 6, and 8: Purl.

back panel

You will make three panels and then sew them together.

With size 9 needles and CC, CO 41 (45, 49, 53) sts. Work stripe pattern and chevron pattern together, decreasing 1 st at each edge every 16th row 4 times. Length should measure approximately 17"/43 cm.

left and right fronts

With size 9 needles and CC, CO 51 (53, 55, 57) sts. Work stripe pattern and chevron pattern together, decreasing 1 st at each edge every 16th row 4 times. Length should measure approximately 17"/43 cm.

sleeves

With size 9 needles and CC, CO 51 (53, 55, 57) sts. Work stripe pattern and chevron pattern together, increasing 1 st at each edge every 16th row 4 times until piece measures 15½ (16, 16½, 16½)"/39.5 (40.5, 42, 42) cm. SHAPE CAP: Continuing in stripe pattern, BO 3 stitches at beginning of next 8 rows. BO remaining stitches loosely.

Skill level | ADVANCED

Sizes

SMALL (Medium, Large, Extra-Large) Instructions are given for smallest size, with larger sizes in parentheses. When only one number is given, it applies to all sizes.

Finished measurements

CHEST 36 (40, 44, 48)"/91 (101.5, 112, 122) cm
LENGTH 24 (24½, 25, 26½)"/61 (62.5, 63.5, 67) cm

Materials

2 skeins Trendsetter Yarns Dune (41% mohair, 29% nylon, 30% acrylic: 1¾ oz/50 g; 90 yds/81 m) in #68 Cream (A), #80 Gold (B), #110 Light Green (C), #45 Green (D), and #100 Dark Green (E)
1 skein each of Trendsetter Yarns Dune in #1 Grey (F) and #111 Rose (G)
CC: 4 (4, 5, 5) GGH Samoa (50% cotton, 50% polyacyl: 1¾ oz/50 g; 104 yds/95 m) in #16 Black

Needles

Size 9 (5.5 mm) and size 9 circular or size needed to obtain gauge

Gauge

16 sts and 20 rows = 4"/10 cm over St st
To save time, take time to check gauge.

top

With size 9 needles and CC, CO 40 (44, 48, 52) sts.
Row 1: Knit, placing marker before and after the center 2 sts.
Row 2: With CC, knit.
Row 3: With E, K to 2 sts before marker, k2tog back, slip marker, k2, k2tog, slip marker, knit to end.
Row 4 and all even rows: Knit.
Repeat rows 1–4 three times, then change to F until 2 sts are left. BO.

Elizabeth

(CONTINUED)

yoke

With size 9 needles and CC, CO 19 (21, 23, 25) sts, knit 2 rows with CC and two rows with E. Repeat 2 rows of each color, and *at the same time*, decrease 1 st at each edge every 4th row 6 times, then increase 1 st at each edge every 4th row 6 times. Then, BO 8 (9, 10, 12) sts at right edge only and dec 1 st at left edge every 4th row 2 times, then every 6th row 4 times. For medium, large, and extra-large sizes work (6,

10, 14) more rows. (You are at the middle of your back.) Reverse shaping: Inc 1 st at left edge every 6th row 4 times, then every 4th row 2 times. CO 8 sts at beg of right edge, then dec 1 st at each edge every 4th row 6 times, then inc 1 st at each edge every 4th row 6 times and BO.

finishing

Sew the chevron panels of the back together. Sew diamonds to chevron bodies. Then sew

yoke to diamonds. Sew side seams (see page 15). NECK BAND: With size 9 circular needles and CC, and starting 5"/12.5 cm down from right shoulder, pick up and knit 12 (12, 16, 16) sts, 24 sts from back and 12 (12, 16, 16) sts down left front. Work in garter st, pick up 3 sts more down each front 8 times. Then pick up 48 sts down to the bottom of each front for front bands. Knit one row. BO loosely. Sew on sleeves.

SLEEVE

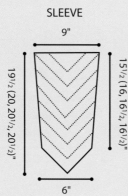

9"

19½ (20, 20½, 20½)"

15½ (16, 16½, 16½)"

6"

FRONT

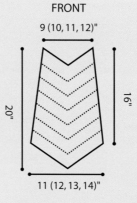

9 (10, 11, 12)"

20"

16"

11 (12, 13, 14)"

BACK

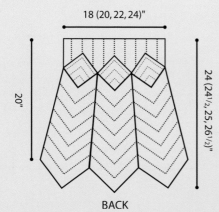

18 (20, 22, 24)"

20"

24 (24½, 25, 26½)"

YOKE

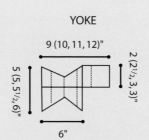

9 (10, 11, 12)"

5 (5, 5½, 6)"

2 (2½, 3, 3)"

6"

DIAMOND

6x6"

to sleeve or not to sleeve

We begin with Anne, a simple sleeveless tank done in stockinette stitch, that can be worn under a jacket or on its own. Then, with a slight change of neckline and the addition of short peek-a-boo sleeves, Anne gets recast as Terri. Switch to seed stitch, a boat neck, and seductive long peek-a-boo sleeves, and it's Lynn, ready to take on the day.

Skill level | EASY

Sizes

SMALL (Medium, Large, Extra-Large)
Instructions are given for smallest size, with
larger sizes in parentheses. When only one
number is given, it applies to all sizes.

Finished measurements

CHEST 37 (40, 44, 47)"/94 (101.5, 112,
119.5) cm
LENGTH 20½ (22, 22½, 24)"/52 (56, 57, 61)
cm

Materials

4 (5, 5, 6) skeins Tahki Stacy Charles S. Charles
Collection Cancun (68% polyester, 8% cotton,
10% nylon, 14% viscose: 1¾ oz/50 g; 93 yds/82
m) in #92
3 (4, 5, 5) skeins Tahki Stacy Charles Filatura
Di Crosa Millefili Fine (100% cotton: 1¾ oz/50
g; 136 yds/122 m) in #164 yellow

Needles

Size 10.5 (6.5 mm) or size needed to obtain
gauge
Size H-8 crochet hook

Gauge

12 sts and 16 rows = 4"/10 cm over St st
To save time, take time to check gauge.

Choose not to sleeve? Then work up this classic
tank in a very easy, versatile pattern. This is a
perfect project for beginners since the back of Anne
can serve as the foundation piece for almost endless
variations of any number of sweaters.

DESIGNER'S NOTES

You know All the leftover thin novelty yarn you have? Well, just get a solid-colored sport-weight yarn to run all your leftovers with. Have fun changing the novelty yarns and creating your own one-of-a-kind tanks.

INSTRUCTIONS

back and front

With size 10.5 needles, CO 56 (62, 68, 74) sts.
Work in St st until piece measures 13 (14, 14,
15)"/33 (35.5, 35.5, 38) cm.
SHAPE ARMHOLE: BO 3 (3, 4, 4) sts at
beg of next 2 rows, then dec 1 st at each edge
every other row 5 (6, 7, 8) times. Work even
until piece measures 17 (18, 18½, 19)"/43
(45.5, 47, 48.5) cm.
SHAPE NECK: Work 13 (15, 15, 15) sts,
join a second ball of yarn, and BO center 14
(14, 14, 16) sts; work to end of row. Working

both sides at once, BO at each neck edge 2 (2,
3, 3) sts once, then dec 1 st every other row 1
(2, 2, 3) times. Work even on remaining 10
(11, 10, 11) sts until piece measures 20½ (22,
22½, 24)"/52 (56, 57, 61) cm. BO loosely.

finishing

Sew shoulder and side seams (see page 15).
NECK BAND: With right side facing and
size H-8 crochet hook, single crochet around
neckline, armhole, and base of tank. Then
work one row of shrimp st.

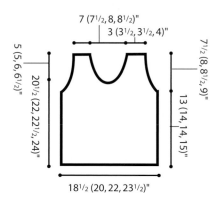

7 (7½, 8, 8½)"
3 (3½, 3½, 4)"
5 (5, 6, 6½)"
20½ (22, 22½, 24)"
7½ (8, 8½, 9)"
13 (14, 14, 15)"
18½ (20, 22, 23½)"

Cut-out short sleeves
that tie above the
elbow and a rounded,
scooped neck are
the features of this
version of the tradi-
tional tank. For those
of you who want a
plain T-shirt,
simply continue
in stockinette stitch,
omitting the cutout
pattern on the sleeves.

Terri

INSTRUCTIONS

back

With size 8 needles, CO 64 (70, 74, 78) sts. Work in K1, P1 ribbing for 1"/2.5 cm. Change to size 10.5 needles and work in St st until piece measures 13 (14, 14, 15)"/33 (35.5, 35.5, 38) cm.

SHAPE ARMHOLE: BO 3 (3, 4, 4) sts at beg of next 2 rows, then dec 1 st at each edge every other row 5 (6, 7, 8) times. Work even until piece measures 20½ (22, 22½, 24)"/52 (56, 57, 61) cm. BO.

front

With size 8 needles, CO 64 (70, 74, 78) sts. Work in K1, P1 ribbing for 1"/2.5 cm. Change to size 10.5 needles, and work in St st until piece measures 13 (14, 14, 15)"/33 (35.5, 35.5, 38) cm.

SHAPE ARMHOLE: BO 3 (3, 4, 4) sts at beg of next 2 rows, then dec 1 st at each edge every other row 5 (6, 7, 8) times. Work even

until piece measures 14 (15, 16, 16½)"/35.5 (38, 40.5, 42) cm.

SHAPE NECK: Work 17 (19, 18, 19) sts, join a second ball of yarn, and BO center 14 (14, 16, 16) sts; work to end of row. Working both sides at once, BO at each neck edge 2 (3 3, 3) sts once, then dec 1 st every other row 1 (2, 1, 1) times. Work even on remaining 14 (14, 13, 13) sts until piece measures same as back. BO loosely.

sleeves

With size 10.5 needles, CO 44 (46, 48, 52) sts. Work in St st for 4 rows. BO 26 sts at beg of next row. Then dec 1 st at beg of right-side row (this is your inside cut-out) every other row 4 (4, 5, 5) times. Work 4 rows even, then increase 1 st every other row 4 (4, 5, 5) times and *at the same time,* inc 1 st at end of right-side row every 4th row 2 (2, 3, 3) times until piece measures 4 (4½, 5, 6)"/10 (12, 12.5, 15) cm.

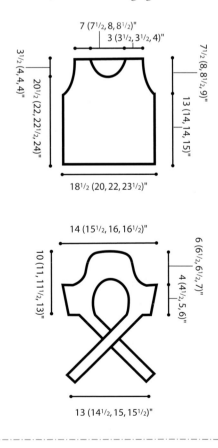

Skill level | INTERMEDIATE

Sizes

SMALL (Medium, Large, Extra-Large) Instructions are given for smallest size, with larger sizes in parentheses. When only one number is given, it applies to all sizes.

Finished measurements

CHEST 39 (43, 45, 48)"/99 (109, 114, 122) cm
LENGTH 20½ (22, 22½, 24)"/52 (56, 57, 61) cm

Materials

7 (8, 9, 10) skeins Plymouth Yarn Company Odyssey Glitz (60% nylon, 37% wool, 3% lamé: 1¾ oz/50 g; 66 yds/60 m) in #912 Geranium

Needles

Size 8 (5 mm) and size 10.5 (6.5 mm) or size needed to obtain gauge
Size J-10 crochet hook

Gauge

13 sts and 16 rows = 4"/10 cm over St st
To save time, take time to check gauge.

Terri
(CONTINUED)

SHAPE CAP: BO 3 (3, 4, 5) sts at beg of wrong-side row. Then, dec 1 st at beg of WS edge every other row 3 times. Put sts on holder. Work other half of sleeve, reversing all shaping.

JOIN: Continue in St st dec 1 st at each edge every other row 4 (4, 6, 6) times. Then BO 2 sts at beg of next 4 rows. BO remaining sts loosely.

finishing
Sew shoulder seams together (see page 15). With size J-10 hook, single crochet around neck, making loop for button back. Sew on sleeves, sew side seams, and sew on button (see pages 15–16).

Lynn is a pretty pullover with long sleeves that have playful open-hole detailing down the sides. It is knitted in seed stitch, which gives the sweater great texture. The back and front are bound off for a boat neck by sewing up the shoulder seams until you reach the desired width.

DESIGNER'S NOTE

The seed stitch is one of my favorite textural stitches, and it's so easy. All you do is knit the purl stitches and purl the knit stitches, following the pattern.

If you'd rather make Lynn with closed sleeves, omit the opening pattern entirely and continue in seed stitch, or make just one opening if that's your preference.

INSTRUCTIONS

front

With size 8 needles, CO 64 (70, 74, 78) sts. Work in K1, P1 ribbing for 1"/2.5 cm. Change to size 10.5 needles and work in seed st until piece measures 15 (16, 17, 18)"/38 (40.5, 43, 45.5) cm.

SHAPE ARMHOLE: BO 3 (3, 4, 4) sts at beg of next 2 rows, then dec 1 st at each edge every other row 5 (6, 7, 8) times. Work even until piece measures 22½ (24, 25½, 27)"/57 (61, 64, 68.5) cm. BO loosely.

back

Same as Front.

sleeves

With size 10.5 needles, CO 32 (32, 32, 34) sts. Work in seed st for 4 rows, then BO 18 sts at beg of next row. Then dec 1 st at beg of right-side row every other row 4 (4, 5, 5) times. Work 2 rows even, then inc 1 st every other row 4 (4, 5, 5) times *and at the same time,* inc 1 st at end of right-side row every 6th row 2 times. Put sts on holder. Work other half of sleeve,

reversing all shaping. Join, continue in seed st; inc 1 st at each edge every 8th row 2 (3, 3, 4) times *at the same time.* When piece measures 8"/20.5 cm for second cut-out and 14"/35.5 cm for the third cut-out, BO center 2 sts, attach new ball of yarn, and work to end. Dec 1 st at inside edges every other row 4 (4, 5, 5) times, then inc 1 st at inside edges every other row 4 (4, 5, 5) times.

SHAPE CAP: When piece measures 16 (16½, 16½, 17)"/40.5 (42, 42, 43) cm, BO 3 (3, 4, 5) sts at beg of wrong-side row. Then, dec 1 st at beginning of wrong-side edge every other row 3 times. Continue in St st dec 1 st at each edge every other row 4 (4, 6, 6) times. Then BO 2 sts at beg of next 4 rows. BO remaining sts loosely.

finishing

Sew shoulders, leaving a 9-, 10-, or 11-inch/ 23-, 25.5-, or 28-cm opening (this is a personal thing); sew sleeves and side seams (see page 15).

Skill level | INTERMEDIATE

Sizes

SMALL (Medium, Large, Extra-Large) Instructions are given for smallest size, with larger sizes in parentheses. When only one number is given, it applies to all sizes.

Finished measurements

CHEST 37 (40, 42, 45)"/94 (101.5, 106.5, 114) cm
LENGTH 22½ (24, 25½, 27)"/57 (61, 64, 68.5) cm

Materials

6 (7, 7, 8) skeins Lion Brand Yarn Wool-Ease Chunky (80% acrylic, 20% wool: 5 oz/140 g; 153 yds/140 m) in #107 Bluebell

Needles

Size 8 (5 mm) and size 10.5 (6.5 mm) or size needed to obtain gauge
Size H-8 crochet hook

Gauge

14 sts and 18 rows = 4"/10 cm over St st
To save time, take time to check gauge.

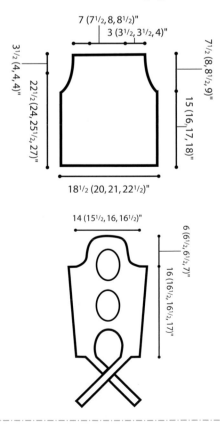

hoods & ribbing

As any fashion star will tell you, it's the details that make the garment. For instance, regardless of whether you actually wear the hood on a sweater, such as the one on Camille, or leave it down, hoods are an attractive and practical knitted detail. One of the most popular details for knitwear is the rib stitch, used as a large ribbed border on both Camille and Emily and as the overall pattern for Mary.

Camille is a hooded sleeveless jacket with a zip-front opening and wide ribbing that starts at the waist and ends at the hips. This adaptable top would be sensational worn on its own to top jeans or as a vest over a long-sleeved tee.

Camille

DESIGNER'S NOTES

By changing the yarn, you can create different looks for different occasions. Knit this in black velvet for a night at the opera. Or picture it in fluffy angora for a Saturday of antique shopping. Work it with two strands of Lion Brand Fun Fur, and you have a faux fur vest to wear when sipping hot toddies après-ski.

INSTRUCTIONS

back

With size 9 needles, and 1 strand each of A and B, CO 63 (69, 75, 81) sts. Work in garter rib as follows: Row 1: Knit. Row 2: *K3, p3*, repeat from *, end k3. Repeat rows 1 and 2 until piece measures 5 (5, 6, 6)"/12.5 (12.5, 15, 15) cm. Change to size 10 needles, and work in St st until piece measures 13 (14, 15, 15)"/33 (35.5, 38, 38) cm.

SHAPE ARMHOLE: BO 4 (4, 5, 6) sts at beg of next 2 rows, then dec 1 st at each edge every other row 4 (4, 5, 6) times. 55 (61, 65, 69) sts. When piece measures 20½ (22, 22½, 24)"/ 52 (56, 57, 61) cm. BO loosely.

front

RIGHT SIDE: With size 9 needles, CO 36 (39, 42, 45) sts. Work in garter rib as follows: Row 1: Knit, Row 2: *K3, P3*, end k3 until piece measures 5 (5, 6, 6)"/12.5 (12.5, 15, 15) cm. Change to size 10 needles, and keep last 3 sts in garter st for front band. Continue until

piece measures 13 (14, 15, 15)"/33 (35.5, 38, 38) cm.

SHAPE ARMHOLE: BO 4 (4, 5, 6) sts at beg of next 2 rows, then dec 1 st at side edge every other row 4 (4, 5, 6) times. When piece measures 17 (19, 19½, 20½)"/48.5 (51, 53.5, 53.5) cm. BO.

SHAPE NECK: At beg of neck edge place 8 sts onto holder, then dec 1 st every other row 4 (5, 6, 6) times. When piece measures same as back, BO remaining 16 (18, 18, 19) sts.

LEFT SIDE: Reverse shaping for left front, keeping the first 3 sts in garter st for band.

finishing

Sew shoulder seams tog and sew side seams (see page 15).

hood

With size 9 needles and RS facing, knit 8 sts from holder, pick up 11 (11, 12, 12) sts up front, 24 (24, 26, 26) sts from back, and 11 (11, 12, 12) sts down front, then knit 8 sts

Skill level | INTERMEDIATE

Sizes

SMALL (Medium, Large, Extra-Large) Instructions are given for smallest size, with larger sizes in parentheses. When only one number is given, it applies to all sizes.

Finished measurements

CHEST 37 (40, 42, 45)"/94 (101.5, 106.5, 114) cm
LENGTH 20½ (22, 22½, 24)"/52 (56, 57, 61) cm

Materials

A: 5 (6, 7, 8) skeins Great Adirondack Yarns Frills (100% rayon crepe: 1¾ oz/50 g; 100 yds/91 m) in Marble
B: 1 (1, 2, 2) skeins Great Adirondack Yarns Seabreeze (100% rayon: 3½ oz/100 g; 475 yds/425 m) in Songbird
18- to 20-inch/45.5- to 51-cm separating zipper
Sewing needle and thread

Needles

Size 9 (5.5 mm) and size 10 (6 mm) or size needed to obtain gauge

Gauge

16 sts and 20 rows = 4"/10 cm over St st
To save time, take time to check gauge.

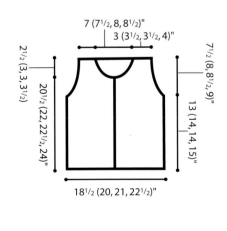

7 (7½, 8, 8½)"
3 (3½, 3½, 4)"
2½ (3, 3, 3½)"
20½ (22, 22½, 24)"
7½ (8, 8½, 9)"
13 (14, 14, 15)"
18½ (20, 21, 22½)"

from holder–62 (62, 66, 66) sts. Follow in pattern for hood.

Row 1: Knit.

Row 2 and all even rows: K3, Purl to the last 3 sts, k3.

Row 3: K30 (30 , 31, 31) sts, place marker, m1, k2 (2, 4, 4) sts, m1, place marker, k30 (30, 31, 31) sts. Now increase 1 st after first marker, and before 2nd marker every other row 4 more times. Work even in St st for 14 rows, keeping first 3 and last 3 sts in garter st. Then

dec 1 st after first marker, and before 2nd marker every other row 5 times. Work 30 (30, 32, 32) sts, leaving the remaining 30 (30, 32, 32) sts. Fold in half inside out and work a three-needle BO. Sew zipper in place. Using a sewing needle, baste zipper in place. Turn the garment inside out and whipstitch the edges of the zipper to the garment. Reinforce the top and the bottom of the zipper with a few extra stitches.

Deep ribbing and high side slits are only two of the features of this young-at-heart polo shirt. Using Camille's back, a half zipper, and a ribbed collar in place of a hood, this updated polo is a must-have for your weekend wardrobe.

Emily

INSTRUCTIONS

back

With size 9 needles, CO 63 (69, 75, 81) sts.
Work in garter rib as follows: Row 1: Knit.
Row 2: *K3, p3*, repeat from *, end k3. Repeat
rows 1 and 2 until piece measures 7 (7, 8,
8)"/18 (18, 20.5, 20.5) cm. Change to size 10
needles, and work in St st until piece measures
13 (14, 15, 15)"/33 (35.5, 38, 38) cm.
SHAPE ARMHOLE: BO 4 (4, 5, 6) sts at
beg of next 2 rows, then dec 1 st at each edge
every other row 4 (4, 5, 6) times, for 55 (61, 65,
69) sts. BO loosely when piece measures 20½
(22, 22½, 24)"/52 (56, 57, 61) cm.

front

With size 9 needles, CO 63 (69, 75, 81) sts.
Work in garter rib as follows: Row 1: Knit.
Row 2: *K3, p3*, repeat from *, end k3 until
piece measures 7 (7, 8, 8)"/18 (18, 20.5, 20.5)
cm. Change to size 10 needles, and work in St
st until piece measures 10 (11, 12, 13)"/25.5
(28, 30.5, 33) cm, divide in half, work 31 (34,
37, 40) sts, join a second ball of yarn, and BO
center stitch; work to end of row. Work both
sides at once until piece measures 13 (14, 15,
15)"/33 (35.5, 38,38) cm.
SHAPE ARMHOLE: BO 4 (4, 5, 6) sts at
beg of next 2 rows, then dec 1 st at each edge
every other row 4 (4, 5, 6) times.

SHAPE NECK: When piece measures 17
(19, 19½, 20½)"/ 43 (48, 50, 52) cm, at beg of
each neck edge place 8 sts onto holder, then
dec 1 st every other row 4 (5, 6, 6) times.
When piece measures same as back, BO
remaining 11 (13, 13, 14) sts loosely.

finishing

Sew shoulder seams together and sew side
seams (see page 15).

collar

With size 9 needles and RS facing, knit 8 sts
from holder, pick up 11 (11, 12, 12) sts from
front, 25 (25, 29, 29) sts from back, and 11
(11, 12, 12) sts down front and then knit 8 sts
from holder 63—(69, 69, 69) sts.
Row 1: Knit.
Row 2 and all even rows: K3, P3, to the last 3
sts, k3. Repeat rows 1 and 2 until collar measures 5"/12.5 cm. BO loosely. Single crochet
with size H-8 crochet hook around front slit.
Sew zipper in place. Using a sewing needle,
baste zipper in place. Turn the garment inside
out and whipstitch the edges of the zipper to
the garment. Reinforce the top and the bottom of the zipper with a few extra stitches.

Skill level EASY

Sizes

SMALL (Medium, Large, Extra-Large)
Instructions are given for smallest size, with
larger sizes in parentheses. When only one
number is given, it applies to all sizes.

Finished measurements

CHEST 37 (40, 42, 45)"/94 (101.5, 106.5, 114) cm
LENGTH 20½ (22, 22½, 24)"/52 (56, 57, 61) cm

Materials

8 (9, 10, 12) skeins Rowan Yarns Cotton Rope
(55% cotton, 45% acrylic: 1¾ oz/50 g; 63
yds/58 m) in #061 Squash
6-inch/15-cm zipper
2 small stitch holders
Sewing needle

Needles

Size 9 (5.5 mm) and size 10 (6 mm) or size
needed to obtain gauge
Size H-8 crochet hook

Gauge

14 sts and 18 rows = 4"/10 cm over St st
To save time, take time to check gauge.

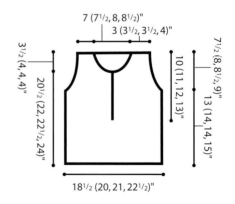

Mary

The stylish V-neck T-shirt doesn't get any better than this. Executed in a shiny, textured, variegated rayon/poly yarn, the bold ribbing pattern of Camille turns subtle here, running through the entire garment. Mary drapes beautifully, never clings, refuses wrinkles, and packs like a dream.

INSTRUCTIONS

back

With size 9 needles CO 63 (69, 75, 81) sts. Work in garter rib as follows: Row 1: Knit. Row 2: *K3, p3*, repeat from *, end k3. Repeat rows 1 and 2 for pattern. Work until piece measures 13 (14, 15, 15)"/33 (35.5, 38, 38) cm. SHAPE ARMHOLE: BO 4 (4, 5, 6) sts at beg of next 2 rows, then dec 1 st at each edge every other row 3 (3, 4, 5) times. BO loosely when piece measures 20½ (22, 22½, 24)"/52 (56, 61, 61) cm.

front

With size 9 needles CO 63 (69, 75, 81) sts. Work in garter rib as follows: Row 1: Knit. Row 2: *K3, p3*, repeat from *, end k3. Repeat rows 1 and 2 for pattern. Work until piece measures 13 (14, 15, 15)"/33 (35.5, 38, 38) cm. Work 31 (34, 37, 40) sts. BO 1 st, attach new skein of yarn, and work remaining 31 (34, 37, 40) sts. Keeping in pattern, dec 1 st at each

neck edge every 4th row 10 (11, 12, 12) times, until piece measures 13 (14, 15, 15)"/33 (35.5, 38, 38) cm. *At the same time:* SHAPE ARMHOLE: BO 4 (4, 5, 6) sts at beg of next 2 rows, then dec 1 st at each edge every other row 3 (3, 4, 5) times. BO loosely when piece measures 20½ (22, 22½, 24)"/52 (56, 57, 61) cm.

sleeves

With size 9 needles CO 45 (51, 51, 57) sts. Work in garter rib pattern for 1½"/3.8 cm. SHAPE ARMHOLE: BO 3 (4, 4, 5) sts at beg of next 2 rows, then dec 1 st at each edge every other row 10 (11, 12, 12) times. Then BO 2 sts at beg of next 4 rows. BO remaining 11 (13, 13, 15) sts.

finishing

Sew shoulder seams together; sew sleeves and side seams (see page 15).

Skill level | EASY

Sizes

SMALL (Medium, Large, Extra-Large) Instructions are given for smallest size, with larger sizes in parentheses. When only one number is given, it applies to all sizes.

Finished measurements

CHEST 37 (40, 42, 45)"/94 (101.5, 106.5, 114) cm
LENGTH 20½ (22, 22½, 24)"/52 (56, 57, 61) cm

Materials

6 (7, 8, 10) skeins Tahki Stacy Charles S. Charles Collection Posh (50% viscose, 40% polyester, 10% polyamide; 1¾ oz/50 g; 81 yds/72 m) in #9 Black

Needles

Size 9 (5.5 mm) or size needed to obtain gauge

Gauge

14 sts and 17 rows = 4"/10 cm over St st
To save time, take time to check gauge.

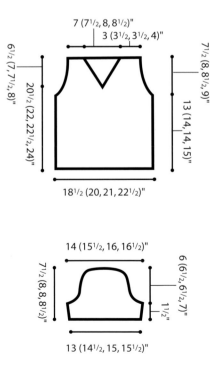

cables galore

Cables, used in a variety of ways, can create eye-popping spiraling effects of both texture and contrast. Of the following rolled-neck and mock-turtleneck sweaters, Cece demonstrates how just a few strategically placed cables can be used to bring interest to the yoke; Cecilia's long, vertical cables establish the overall pattern; and Leah's cables are accented with ribbon woven into the pattern.

Cece

The cabled shell is just right for those spring days when the sun is shining and a breeze is teasing. Three simple cables radiate out and down from the rolled mock turtleneck to highlight the sweater's yoke and recessed armholes, and bring attention to the shoulders.

Skill level | INTERMEDIATE

Sizes

SMALL (Medium, Large, Extra-Large) Instructions are given for smallest size, with larger sizes in parentheses. When only one number is given, it applies to all sizes.

Finished measurements

CHEST 36 (39, 43, 47)"/91.5 (99, 109, 119) cm
LENGTH 20½ (22, 22½, 24)"/52 (56, 57, 61) cm

Materials

3 (4, 5, 5) skeins Plymouth Yarn Company Fantasy Naturale (100% mercerized cotton: 3½ oz/100 g; 140 yds/126 m) in #8176 Ivory

Needles

Size 9 (5.5 mm) and size 7 (4.5 mm) or size needed to obtain gauge
Cable needle
Size H-8 crochet hook

Gauge

17 sts and 14 rows = 4"/10 cm over St st
To save time, take time to check gauge.

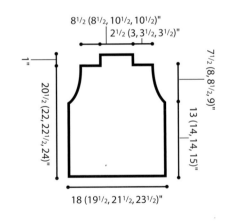

INSTRUCTIONS

C4 = Slip 2 sts onto cn, hold in back, k2, k2 from cn.

back and front

With size 7 needles, CO 76 (84, 92, 100) sts. Work in K1, P1 ribbing for 1"/2.5 cm. Change to size 9 needles and St st and dec 1 st at each edge every 8th row 3 times. Then when piece measures 8 (9, 10, 11)"/20.5 (23, 25.5, 28) cm, inc 1 st at each edge every 8th row 3 times.
SHAPE ARMHOLE: When piece measures 13 (14, 14, 15)"/33 (35.5, 35.5, 38) cm, BO 4 sts at beg of next 2 rows, then dec 1 st at each edge every other row 4 (4, 5, 6) times 60 (68, 76, 80) sts.

start cable pattern

Row 1: Knit.
Rows 2 and 4: Purl.
Row 3: *K12 (13, 16, 17) (C4)* repeat from * and k12 (13, 16, 17).

Repeat rows 1–4 for pattern twice, then continue working cable every 4th row, moving side cables 1 st toward the center cable. (Knit 1 st more before first cable, 1 st less between first center cable, 1 st less between center and third cable and 1 st more after third cable than previous cable row.) Continue in pattern until piece measures 20½ (22, 22½, 24)"/52 (56, 57, 61) cm. BO 12 (14, 16, 18) sts at beginning of next two rows. Work even in pattern for 1"/2.5 cm (this is your neck). BO very loosely.

finishing

Sew shoulders and side seams.

arm bands

With RS facing and size H-8 crochet hook, work 1 round of single crochet then 1 round of shrimp st.

Trendy and casual, Cecilia is a long-sleeve version of Cece but features cables used in a totally different manner—running all the way down the garment, in front, on the back, and on the sleeves.

Cecilia

DESIGNER'S NOTES

Variations on Cecilia might be to delete the center cable, add additional cables, or eliminate them altogether for a sleek silhouette. This is my favorite "whatever the weather, wherever I go sweater." The blend of cotton and viscose fiber breathes, and it packs well.

INSTRUCTIONS

C4 = Slip 2 sts onto cn, hold in back, k2, k2 from cn.

back and front

With size 7 needles, CO 76 (84, 92, 100) sts. Work in k1, p1 ribbing for 1"/2.5 cm. Change to size 9 needles and pattern st below.

Row 1: Knit.

Rows 2 and 4: Purl.

Row 3: *K16 (18, 20, 22) (C4)* repeat from * and k16 (18, 20, 22).

Repeat rows 1–4 for pattern. *At the same time,* decrease 1 st at each edge every 8th row 3 times. When piece measures 8 (9, 10, 11)"/20.5 (23, 25.5, 28) cm, increase 1 st at each edge every 8th row 3 times.

SHAPE ARMHOLE: When piece measures 13 (14, 14, 15)"/33 (35.5, 35.5, 38) cm, BO 4 sts at beg of next 2 rows, then dec 1 st at each edge every other row 4 (5, 5, 6) times 60 (66, 76, 80) sts. *At the same time,* continue working cable every 4th row, moving side cables 1 st toward the center cable (knit 1 st more before first cable, 1 st less between first center cable, 1 st less between center and 3rd cable and 1 st more after 3rd cable than previous cable row). Continue in pattern until piece measures

20½ (22, 22½, 24)"/52 (56, 57, 61) cm. BO 12 (14, 16, 18) sts at beginning of next two rows. Work even in pattern for 1"/2.5 cm. BO very loosely.

sleeves

CO 36 (38, 40, 42) sts. Work in k1, p1 ribbing for 1"/2.5 cm.

Row 1: Knit.

Rows 2 and 4: Purl.

Row 3: K16 (17, 18, 19) C4, K16 (17 18, 19).

Repeat rows 1–4 for pattern.

Work in pattern, and *at the same time,* inc 1 st at each end every 6th row 13 (13, 14, 15) times. 62 (64, 68, 72) sts. (*Note: For better seams, work incs 2 sts in from edges.*) Work even until piece measures 16 (16½, 16½, 17)"/40.5 (42, 42, 43) cm.

SHAPE CAP: BO 4 sts at beg of next 2 rows. Then dec 1 st at each edge every other row 13 (13, 14, 15) times. Then BO 2 sts at beginning of next 4 rows. BO remaining 20 (22, 24, 26) sts.

finishing

Sew sleeves and side seams (see page 15).

Skill level | INTERMEDIATE

Sizes

SMALL (Medium, Large, Extra-Large)
Instructions are given for smallest size, with larger sizes in parentheses. When only one number is given, it applies to all sizes.

Finished measurements

CHEST: 36 (39, 43, 47)"/91.5 (99, 109, 119) cm
LENGTH: 20½ (22, 22½, 24)"/52 (56, 57, 61) cm

Materials

11 (12, 13, 15) skeins Tahki Stacy Charles Collection Victoria (60% cotton, 40% viscose: 1¾ oz/50 g; 71 yds/64 m) in #1 Bleach

Needles

Size 9 (5.5 mm) and size 7 (4.5 mm) or size needed to obtain gauge
Cable needle

Gauge

17 sts and 21 rows = 4"/10 cm over St st
To save time, take time to check gauge.

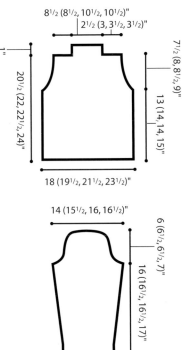

8½ (8½, 10½, 10½)"

2½ (3, 3½, 3½)"

1"

20½ (22, 22½, 24)"

7½ (8, 8½, 9)"

13 (14, 14, 15)"

18 (19½, 21½, 23½)"

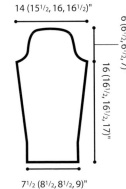

14 (15½, 16, 16½)"

6 (6½, 6½, 7)"

16 (16½, 16½, 17)"

7½ (8½, 8½, 9)"

Leah

On the yoke of this dressy, gold-flecked shell, the cables are almost undetectable until strips of gold ribbon are woven through the spaces between them. To call attention to well-toned shoulders, the armhole decreases are worked a few more times for a more cut-out look.

DESIGNER'S NOTES

This would look fantastic with strips of fur substituted for the ribbon and woven into the cable opening. Yummy!

INSTRUCTIONS

C4 = Slip 2 sts onto cn, hold in back, k2, k2 from cn.

back and front

With size 7 needles, CO 76 (84, 92, 100) sts. Work in K1, P1 ribbing for 1"/2.5 cm. Change to size 9 needles, and St st dec 1 st at each edge every 8th row 3 times. Then when piece measures 8 (9, 10, 11)"/20.5 (23, 25.5, 28) cm, increase 1 st at each edge every 8th row 3 times.

SHAPE ARMHOLE: When piece measures 13 (14, 14, 15)"/33 (35.5, 35.5, 38) cm, BO 4 sts at beg of next 2 rows, then dec 1 st at each edge every other row 4 (4, 5, 6) for the cut-out version dec 6 more times—60 (68, 76, 80) 48 (56, 64, 68) sts. Start cable pattern as follows:
Row 1: Knit.
Rows 2 and 4: Purl.
Row 3: *K12, (13, 16, 17), (C4)* repeat from *

and k12, (13, 16, 17). Repeat rows 1–4 for pattern twice, then continue working cable every 4th row, moving side cables 1 st toward the center cable. (Knit 1 st more before 1st cable, 1 st less between 1st center cable, 1 st less between center and 3rd cable, and 1 st more after 3rd cable than previous cable row.) Continue in pattern until piece measures 20½ (22, 22½, 24)"/52 (56, 57, 61) cm. BO 12 (14, 16, 18) sts at beginning of next two rows. Work even in pattern for 1"/2.5 cm, BO very loosely.

finishing

Sew shoulders and side seams.
ARMBANDS: With RS facing and size H-8 crochet hook, work one round of single crochet then one round of shrimp st.

Skill level | INTERMEDIATE

Sizes
SMALL (Medium, Large, Extra-Large)
Instructions are given for smallest size, with larger sizes in parentheses. When only one number is given, it applies to all sizes.

Finished measurements
CHEST 36 (39, 43, 47)"/91.5 (99, 109, 119) cm
LENGTH 20½ (22, 22½, 24)"/52 (56, 57, 61) cm

Materials
5 (6, 7, 8) skeins Prism Arts Yarn Wild Stuff (88% rayon, 9% nylon, 3% polyester: 2 oz/58 g; 125 yds/113 m) in Lipstick

Needles
Size 9 (5.5 mm) and size 7 (4.5 mm) or size needed to obtain gauge
Size H-8 crochet hook

Gauge
17 sts and 18 rows = 4"/10 cm over St st
To save time, take time to check gauge.

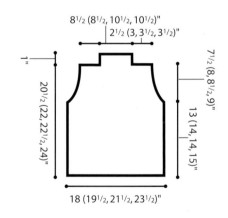

8½ (8½, 10½, 10½)"
2½ (3, 3½, 3½)"
1"
7½ (8, 8½, 9)"
20½ (22, 22½, 24)"
13 (14, 14, 15)"
18 (19½, 21½, 23½)"

sweatshirt to soirée

For projects that offer immediate gratification, these three sweaters should fill the bill. Knit on large needles, they all have the same basic body shape, raglan sleeves, and ribbing at the bottom and at the wrists. But that's where the similarities end. It's in the individual details that this trio is as different as morning, noon, and night.

Cuddly and soft, with
a generous hood and
front hand-warmer
pockets, this is what
every sweatshirt
wishes it could be.
It knits up so
quickly, you'll want
to put it right on and
take a walk in the
park to kick up fallen
autumn leaves.

Judi

Skill level | EASY

Sizes

SMALL (Medium, Large, Extra-Large)
Instructions are given for smallest size, with
larger sizes in parentheses. When only one
number is given, it applies to all sizes.

Finished measurements

CHEST 40 (44, 48, 52)"/94 (101.5, 122, 132) cm
LENGTH 23 (24, 26, 27)"/58.5 (61, 66, 68.5) cm

Materials

13 (14, 15, 16) skeins Tahki Stacy Charles Baby
Tweed (92% wool, 8% viscose: 3½ oz/100 g; 60
yds/55 m) in #03 Baby Blue
4 large stitch holders
2 large stitch markers

Needles

Size 11 (8 mm) straight and circular and size
15 (10 mm) or size needed to obtain gauge

Gauge

8 sts and 10 rows = 4"/10 cm over St st
To save time, take time to check gauge.

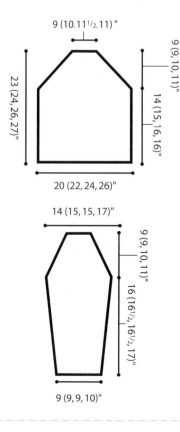

INSTRUCTIONS

front

With size 11 needles, CO 40 (44, 48, 52) sts.
Work in K1, P1 ribbing for 2"/5 cm. Change
to size 15 needles and St st until piece measures 14 (15, 16, 16)"/35.5 (38, 40.5, 40.5) cm.
SHAPE ARMHOLE: BO 2 (2, 2, 3) sts at
beg of next 2 rows. Then dec 1 st at each edge
every other row 9 (10, 11, 12) times. Dec all
raglans as follows:
Row 1: K1, sl1, k1, psso, k to the last 3 sts
k2tog, k1.
Row 2: Purl.
Put remaining 18 (20, 22, 22) sts on a holder.

back

Same as front.

sleeves

With size 11 needles, CO 18 (18, 18, 20) sts.
Work in K1, P1 ribbing for 2"/5 cm. Change
to size 15 needles and St st. *At the same time,
inc 1 st at each end every 6th row 5 (6, 6, 7)
times. (Note: For better seams, work incs 2 sts in
from edges.)* Work even until piece measures
16 (16½, 16½, 17)"/40.5 (42, 42, 43) cm.
SHAPE CAP: BO 2 (2, 2, 3) sts at beg of
next 2 rows. Then dec 1 st at each edge every
other row 9 (10, 11, 12) times. Put remaining
6 (6, 4, 4) sts on a holder.

finishing

Sew raglan and side seams (see page 15).
NECK BAND: With size 11 circular

needles, knit 18 (20, 22, 22) sts on front
holder, put 6 (6, 4, 4) sts on sleeve holder.
Knit 18 (20, 22, 22) sts on back holder, put 6
(6, 4, 4) sts on sleeve holder. Dec 1 st at each
of the 4 raglan seams (knit the last st of one
to the first st of the other piece you have
sewn)—44 (48, 48, 48) sts around neck edge.
Join and work in k1, p1 ribbing for 1"/2.5 cm.
HOOD: BO the center 5 sts. (Remember
you can pick either piece—the front and the
back are exactly the same; count from the
sleeve seam in to find your center.)
Row 1: K1, p1, k1, p1, k10, place marker, k11
(15, 15, 15), place marker, k10, p1, k1, p1, k1.
Row 2: P1, k1, p1, k1, p10, slip marker, p11
(15, 15, 15) slip marker, p10, k1, p1, k1, p1.
Repeat rows 1 and 2 for pattern. Inc 1 st after
first marker and before second marker every
6th row twice. Work in pattern until hood
measures 10"/25.5 cm. Then dec 1 st after
first marker and before second marker. Work
dec row every 6th row 2 more times. When
piece measures 15"/38 cm, work 17 (19, 19,
19) sts, k2 together, leaving the remaining 18
(20, 20, 20) sts. On a spare needle, fold in half
inside-out and work a three-needle BO. With
right sides together, hold the knitting in your
left hand. Place third needle in your right
hand. Insert the right-hand needle into the
first stich of the front needle and then into
the first stitch of the back needle, then knit
the two stitches together *at the same time.*

9 (10, 11½, 11)"

9 (9, 10, 11)"

23 (24, 26, 27)"

14 (15, 16, 16)"

20 (22, 24, 26)"

14 (15, 15, 17)"

9 (9, 10, 11)"

16 (16½, 16½, 17)"

9 (9, 9, 10)"

Judi

(CONTINUED)

Repeat with the next two stitches on the left-hand needle, then bind off in the usual manner loosely. Continue knitting two stitches together from front and back needles, binding off across the row. When one stitch remains on right-hand needle, cut tail and pull through last loop.

POCKET: With size 11 needles, CO 18 (18, 18, 20) sts.

Row 1: K1, p1, k1, p1, k11, p1, k1, p1, k1.

Row 2: P1, k1, p1, k1, p11, k1, p1, k1, p1.

Repeat rows 1 and 2 for pattern. BO when pocket measures 7"/18 cm.

Pin pocket to garment and sew in place.

Here's the same quick-to-knit raglan but with a lush ribbed cowl that will turn heads on and off the slopes. A reverse stockinette stripe set slightly off-center and two pompoms dangling from the cowl add a little pizzazz and keep the knitting exciting.

Susan

INSTRUCTIONS

front

With size 11 needles, CO 40 (44, 48, 52) sts. Work in ribbing for 1½"/3.8 cm. Change to size 15 needles. Work pattern as follows:

Row 1: K12, p5, k23 (27, 31, 35) sts.

Row 2: P23 (27, 31, 35) sts.

Work in pattern until piece measures 14 (15, 16, 16)"/35.5 (38, 40.5 40.5) cm.

SHAPE ARMHOLE: BO 2 (2, 2, 3) sts at beg of next 2 rows. Then dec 1 st at each edge every other row 9 (10, 11, 12) times. Dec all raglans as follows:

Row 1: K1, sl1, k1 psso, k to last 3 sts, k2tog, k1. Put remaining 18 (20, 22, 22) sts on a holder.

Row 2: Purl.

back

With size 11 needles, CO 40 (44, 48, 52) sts. Work in K1, P1 ribbing for 1½"/3.8 cm. Change to size 15 needles and St st until piece measures 14 (15, 16, 16)"/35.5 (38, 40.5, 40.5) cm.

SHAPE ARMHOLE: BO 2 (2, 2, 3) sts at beg of next 2 rows. Then dec 1 st at each edge every other row 9 (10, 11, 12) times. Put remaining 18 (20, 22, 22) sts on a holder.

sleeves

With size 11 needles, CO 18 (18, 18, 20) sts. Work in K1, P1 ribbing for 1½"/3.8 cm. Change to size 15 needles and St st. *At the same time*, inc 1 st at each end every 6th row 5 (6, 6, 7) times. *(Note: For better seams, work incs 2 sts in from edges.)* Work even until piece measures 16 (16½, 16½, 17)"/40.5 (42, 42, 43) cm.

SHAPE CAP: BO 2 (2, 2, 3) sts at beg of next 2 rows. Then dec 1 st at each edge every other row 9 (10, 11, 12) times. Put remaining 6 (6, 4, 4) sts on a holder.

finishing

Sew raglan and side seams (see page 15).

NECK BAND: With size 11 circular needles, knit the 18 (20, 22, 22) sts on front holder, the 6 (6, 4, 4) sts on sleeve holder, the 18 (20, 22, 22) sts on back holder, and the 6 (6, 4, 4) sts on sleeve holder. Dec 1 st at each of the four raglan seams (knit the last st of one to the first st of the other piece you have sewn), for 44 (48, 48, 48) sts around neck edge. Join and work in k1, p1 ribbing for 3"/7.5 cm, keeping the 5 sts in rev St that you did up the front. Then change to size 15 needles. Keep in k1, p1 rib, changing the 5 rev St sts to St st so the purl side shows when folded over. Continue until piece measures 8"/20.5 cm. BO all sts loosely. With a single strand of yarn, lace up the front reverse St st pattern on the collar and make two pompoms. Buy a pompom maker at any craft or yarn shop (it's the best two-dollar bargain you'll ever find!).

Skill level : EASY

Sizes:

SMALL (medium, large, extra-large) instructions are given for smallest size, with larger sizes in parentheses. When only one number is given, it applies to all sizes.

finished measurements

CHEST 40 (44, 48, 52)"/101.5 (112, 122, 132) cm

LENGTH 23 (24, 26, 27)"/58.5 (61, 66, 68.5) cm

Materials

6 (7, 8, 9) skeins Lion Brand Wool-Ease Thick & Quick (80% acrylic, 20% wool: 6 oz/170 g; 108 yds/99 m) in #099 Fisherman

Needles

Size 11 (8 mm) straight and circular and size 15 (10 mm) or size needed to obtain gauge

Gauge

8 sts and 10 rows = 4"/10 cm over St st
To save time, take time to check gauge.

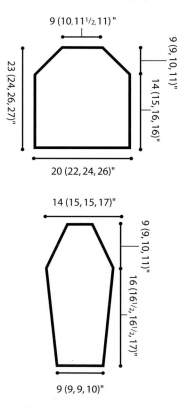

Jacki

This dressy raglan sweater was done with a combination of two novelty yarns. The sweeping come-hither neckline gives it just the right amount of sex appeal without being revealing. Although the gauge is large, it's a remarkably light and comfortable sweater.

INSTRUCTIONS

front

With size 11 needles and one strand of each yarn, CO 40 (44, 48 52) sts. Work in k1, p1 ribbing for 2"/5 cm. Change to size 15 needles and St st until piece measures 14 (15, 16, 16)"/35.5 (38, 40.5, 40.5) cm.

SHAPE ARMHOLE: BO 2 (2, 2, 3) sts at beg of next 2 rows. Then dec 1 st at each edge every other row 8 (9, 10, 10) times. Dec all raglans as follows:

Row 1: K1, sl1, k1, psso k to the last 3 sts k2tog, k1. Put remaining 20 (22, 24, 26) sts on a holder.

Row 2: Purl.

back

Same as Front.

sleeves

With size 11 needles and one strand of each yarn, CO 18 (18, 18, 20) sts. Work in K1, P1 ribbing for 2"/5 cm. Change to size 15 needles and St st. *At the same time,* inc 1 st at each end every 6th row 5 (6, 6, 7) times. *(Note: For better seams, work incs 2 sts in from edges.)* Work even until piece measures 16 (16½, 16½, 17)"/40.5 (42, 42, 43) cm.

SHAPE CAP: BO 2 (2, 2, 3) sts at beg of next 2 rows. Then dec 1 st at each edge every other row 8 (9, 9, 10) times. Put remaining 8 sts on a holder.

finishing

Sew raglan and side seams (see page 15).

NECK BAND: With size 11 circular needles and one strand of each yarn, knit the 20 (22, 24, 26) sts on front holder, the 8 sts on sleeve holder, the 20 (22, 24, 26) sts on back holder, and the 8 sts on sleeve holder. Join and work in K1, P1 ribbing 56 (60, 64, 68) sts around neck edge. Join and work in K1, P1 ribbing for 6"/15 cm. BO all sts loosely.

Skill level | EASY

Sizes

SMALL (Medium, Large, Extra-Large)
Instructions are given for smallest size, with larger sizes in parentheses. When only one number is given, it applies to all sizes.

Finished measurements

CHEST 40 (44, 48, 52)"/101.5 (112, 122, 132) cm
LENGTH 23 (24, 26, 27)"/58.5 (61, 66, 68.5) cm

Materials

6 (7, 8, 9) skeins Berroco Yarn Optik (48% cotton, 21% acrylic, 20% mohair, 8% metallic, 3% polyester: 1¾ oz/50 g; 87 yds/79 m) in #4951 Monsoon

5 (6, 7, 8) skeins Trendsetter Yarns Dune (41% mohair, 29% nylon, 30% acrylic, 1¾ oz/50 g; 90 yds/81 m) in #112 Red

4 large stitch holders

Needles

Size 11 (7 mm) straight and circular and size 15 (10 mm) or size needed to obtain gauge

Gauge

8 sts and 10 rows = 4"/10 cm over St st
To save time, take time to check gauge.

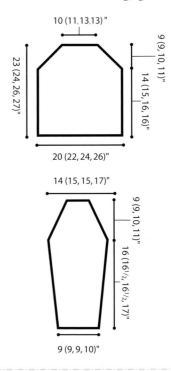

10 (11,13,13)"

23 (24, 26, 27)"

9 (9, 10, 11)"

14 (15,16, 16)"

20 (22, 24, 26)"

14 (15, 15, 17)"

9 (9, 10, 11)"

16 (16½, 16½, 17)"

9 (9, 9, 10)"

ribbons, ruffles & eyelets

Ribbons and ruffles and eyelets, oh my! The three classic shells of this design group are embellished with feminine touches that girls of every age love. Each has a yoke dotted with eyelets, and in two of the sweaters, satiny ombre silk ribbon is woven through the small lacy openings. But these sweaters are not as innocent as they appear. The daring open backs of Dana and Victoria may cause some admiring double-takes, while Phoebe gets its drama from the peek-a-boo eyelets in glittery black yarn, as well as the bare-to-there armholes.

Ribbon stripes are woven through knitted eyelet openings into the yoke pattern of this fitted boat-neck shell. But it's the back—a deep, buttoned opening culminating in a slightly gathered bustle and big cascading bow—that sets this shell apart from the ordinary.

Dana

DESIGNER'S NOTES

I had to show off these shoes, since I went to some trouble to get the match. I ran around trying to find navy espadrilles and couldn't, so I wound up buying a pair that were originally a pink floral print. Then, I went to the Home Depot, bought some spray paint, and sprayed them to match my sweater. Finally, I embellished them with the same silk ribbons I wove into the sweater to make the ankle wrap and toe bows.

INSTRUCTIONS

front

With size 9 needles, CO 68 (74, 80, 86) sts. Work even in St st until piece measures 3½ (4, 4, 5)"/9 (10, 10, 12.5) cm. Dec setup: K1, place marker, k16, place marker, k to last 17 sts, place marker, k16, place marker, k1. Dec on RS 1 st after the first two markers and dec 1 st before the last two markers every 4th row three more times. Work even for 3 (3, 4, 4)"/7.5 (7.5, 10, 10) cm. Then inc 1 st after the first two markers *and* before the last two markers every 4th row four times.

SHAPE ARMHOLE: When piece measures 13 (14, 14, 15)"/33 (35.5, 35.5, 38) cm, BO 3 sts at beg of next 2 rows, then dec 1 st at each edge every other row 4 (5, 5, 6) times 54 (58, 64, 68) sts. *At the same time,* work eyelet pattern:

Row 1: K3 * yo, k2tog, k4 * repeat * end by knitting leftover stitches. (You will be shaping your armholes, so the number of sts will change, and the number of knit stitches here does not matter.)

Rows 2, 4, and 6: Purl.

Row 3: Knit.

Row 5: K1 *(yo, k2tog, k4)* ending with knit stitches.

Repeat rows 1–6 for pattern. Work in pattern until piece measures 17½ (19, 19½, 20)"/44.5 (48.5, 49.5, 51) cm.

Skill level | INTERMEDIATE

Sizes

SMALL (Medium, Large, Extra-Large) Instructions are given for smallest size, with larger sizes in parentheses. When only one number is given, it applies to all sizes.

Finished measurements

CHEST 37 (40, 42, 45)"/94 (101.5, 106,5, 114) cm
LENGTH 20½ (22, 22½, 24)"/52 (56, 57, 61) cm

Materials

9 (10, 12, 13) skeins Great Adirondack Yarns Caribe Irise (95% cotton, 5% polyester: 1¾ oz/50 g; 100 yds/91 m) in Magpie
Matching sewing thread
40"/101.5 cm of 3-inch/7.5-cm hand-dyed Artemis silk ribbon
2 yds/2 m of 1-inch/2.5-cm hand-dyed Artemis silk ribbon
1 1-inch/2.5-cm button
Tapestry needle

Needles

Size 9 (5 mm) or size needed to obtain gauge
Size G-6 crochet hook

Gauge

16 sts and 20 rows = 4"/10 cm over St st
To save time, take time to check gauge.

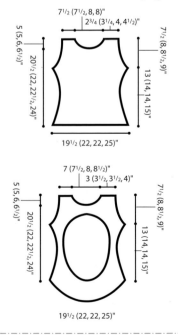

Dana
(CONTINUED)

SHAPE NECK: Work 18 (20, 23, 25) sts. Join a second ball of yarn and BO center 18 sts; work to end of row. Working both sides at once, BO at each neck edge 4 sts once, then dec 1 st every other row 3 times—11 (13, 16, 17) sts remaining each shoulder. Work even until piece measures 20½ (22, 22½, 24)"/52 (56, 57, 61) cm. BO loosely.

back

With size 9 needles, CO 24 (28, 32, 36) sts. Then CO 6 sts at beginning of every row 12 times—96 (100, 104, 108) sts. Work even until piece measures 5 (6, 6, 7)"/12.5 (15, 15, 18) cm. Dec row for gathering back ruffle: K20 (22, 24, 26) sts, k2tog 28 times, k20 (22, 24, 26) sts, for 68 (72, 76, 80) sts. Work even until piece meas-

ures 9 (10, 11, 12)"/23 (25.5, 28, 30.5) cm from CO. Work 26 (27, 29, 30) sts. Join a second ball of yarn and BO center 16 (18, 18, 20) sts; work to end of row. Working both sides at once, dec 1 st every other row 5 (5, 6, 6) times, for 21 (22, 23, 24) sts.

SHAPE ARMHOLE: When piece measures 13 (14, 14, 15)"/33 (35.5, 35.5, 38) cm from side edge, BO 3 sts at beg of next 2 rows, then dec 1 st at each edge every other row 4 (5, 5, 6) times, for 14 (14, 15, 15) sts. At same time, when piece measures 14 (15, 15½, 16)"/35.5 (38, 39.5, 40.5) cm, inc 1 st at inside edge every 4th row 15 (16, 17, 18) times. Work even on remaining 29 (30, 32, 33) sts. Work even until piece measures 20½ (22, 22½, 24)"/52 (56, 57, 61) cm. BO loosely.

finishing

Sew side and shoulder seams (see page 15). With size G-6 crochet hook, single crochet (see pages 15–16) around entire garment. Make a loop for buttonhole at the top of the back neck. Weave in silk ribbons, and make big bow in the back gather to fit.

With tapestry needle, weave in the 1-inch/2.5-cm ribbon in front yoke over and back. Then, with sewing thread, tack the beginning end and the end to the inside of the garment. Take the 3-inch/7.5-cm ribbon, cut in half, and make a big bow. Pull out and fuss, then tack in back. Pick up the phone and go on a date!

Victoria

*Victoria is Dana taken to the extreme. A deep
ruffled ribbon peplum is added to the front, and the
almost-bare back plunges to the waist, where three
tiers of ruffles form a bustle that is finished off
with an extravagant bow.*

DESIGNER'S NOTES

*If the three tiers are too much, you have the option of making only one or two.
You could also do just one ruffle but make it 8"/20.5 cm long, then start the
decrease row pattern so that you have the length of a big bustle without the
thickness of the three tiers.*

INSTRUCTIONS

back

With size 9 needles and CC A, CO 240 sts.
Work in St st for 1½"/3.8 cm. Work short
rows as follows: knit to the last 20 sts; turn,
slip 1 st onto right-hand needle, and purl to
the last 20 sts; turn, slip 1 st onto right-hand
needle, and knit to the last 25 sts; turn, slip 1 st
onto right-hand needle, and purl to the last 25
sts; turn, slip 1 st onto right-hand needle, knit
to the last 30 sts; turn, slip 1 st onto right-hand
needle and purl to the last 30 sts; turn, slip 1 st
onto right-hand needle, and knit to the last 35
sts; turn, slip 1 st onto right-hand needle, and
purl to the last 35 sts; turn, slip 1 st onto right-
hand needle, and knit to the last 40 sts, turn,
slip 1 st onto right-hand needle, and purl to
the last 40 sts; turn, slip 1 st onto right-hand

needle, work to end. Work even on 240 sts for
2 rows. Then decrease 172 (168, 164, 160) sts
evenly across next row, for 68 (72, 76, 80) sts
remaining. Work even until piece measures 6
inches. Work CCB exactly the same until 5
inches and CCC until 4 inches. Join all three
colors and continue in MC until 9 (10, 11,
12)"/23 (25.5, 28, 30.5) cm from CO. Work 26
(27, 29, 30) sts. Join a second ball of yarn. BO
center 16 (18, 18, 20) sts, and work to end of
row. Working both sides at once, dec 1 st
every other row 5 (5, 6, 6) times, for 21 (22, 23,
24) sts remaining.

SHAPE ARMHOLE: When piece meas-
ures 13 (14, 14, 15)"/33 (35.5, 35.5, 38) cm
from side edge, BO 3 sts at beg of next 2 rows,
then dec 1 st at each edge every other row 4 (5,

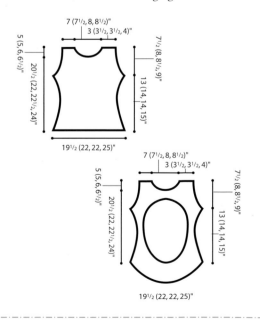

Skill level | INTERMEDIATE

Sizes

SMALL (Medium, Large, Extra-Large)
Instructions are given for smallest size, with
larger sizes in parentheses. When only one
number is given, it applies to all sizes.

Finished measurements

CHEST 37 (40, 42, 45)"/94 (101.5, 106.5, 114) cm
LENGTH 20½ (22, 22½, 24)"/52 (56, 57, 61) cm

Materials

MC: 3 (4, 4, 5) skeins Rowan Yarns Kid Silk
Haze (70% super kid mohair, 30% silk: 1 oz/25
g; 229 yds/210 m) in #590 Ivory
CC A: 1 skein Rowan Yarns Kid Silk Haze in
#581 Meadow
CC B: 1 skein Rowan Yarns Kid Silk Haze in
#580 Grace
40"/101.5 cm of 3-inch/7.5-cm hand-dyed
Artemis silk ribbon
2 yds/2 m of 1-inch/2.5-cm hand-dyed
Artemis silk ribbon
1 1-inch/2.5-cm button

Needles

Size 9 (5.5 mm) or size needed to obtain gauge

Gauge

16 sts and 20 rows = 4"/10 cm over St st
To save time, take time to check gauge.

5, 6) times, for 14 (14, 15, 15) sts. *At the same time,* when piece measures 14 (15, 15½, 16)"/35.5 (38, 39.5 40.5) cm, inc 1 st at inside edge every 4th row 15 (16, 17, 18) times. Work even on remaining 29 (30, 32, 33) sts. Work even until piece measures 20½ (22, 22½, 24)"/52 (56, 57, 61) cm. BO loosely.

front

With size 9 needles and MC, CO 68 (74, 80, 86) sts. Work even in St st until piece measures 3½ (4, 4, 5)"/9 (10, 10, 12.5) cm. Dec setup on wrong-side row: P1, place marker, p16, place marker, purl to last 17 sts, place marker, p16, place marker, p1. On right-side row, dec 1 st after the first two markers and dec 1 st before the last two markers every 4th row three times. Work even for 3 (3, 4, 4)"/7.5 (7.5, 10, 10) cm. Then inc 1 st after the first two markers and inc 1 st before the last two markers every 4th row three times.

SHAPE ARMHOLE: When piece measures 13 (14, 14, 15)"/33 (35.5, 35.5, 38) cm, BO 3 sts at beg of next 2 rows, then dec 1 st at each edge every other row 4 (5, 5, 6) times, for 54 (58, 64, 68) sts. *At the same time,* work eyelet pattern:

Row 1: K3 * yo, k2tog, k4 * repeat * and end by knitting leftover stitches. (You will be shaping your armholes, so the number of sts will change, and the number of knit stitches here does not matter.)

Rows 2, 4, and 6: Purl.

Row 3: Knit.

Row 5: K1 *(yo, k2tog, k4)* ending with knit stitches.

Repeat rows 1–6 for pattern. Work in pattern until piece measures 17½ (19, 19½, 20)"/44.5 (48.5, 49.5 51) cm.

SHAPE NECK: Work 18 (20, 23, 25) sts. Join a second ball of yarn and BO center 18 sts; work to end of row. Working both sides

at once, BO at each neck edge 4 sts once, then dec 1 st every other row 3 times—11 (13, 16, 17) sts remaining each shoulder. Work even until piece measures 20½ (22, 22½, 24)"/52 (56, 57, 61) cm. BO.

finishing

Sew shoulder and side seams (see page 15). NECK BAND: With RS facing, single crochet around neck. Tie on 8 inches/20.5 cm of a 1-inch/2.5-cm ribbon on the top of each side of back neck for the closure, and have fun with as many bows on your bum as you like. Weave in the ribbon on the front. With tapestry needle, weave in the 1-inch/2.5-cm ribbon in front yoke over and back. Then, with sewing thread, tack the beginning end and the end to the inside of the garment. Take the 3-inch/7.5-cm ribbon, cut in half, and make a big bow. Pull out and fuss, then tack in back.

Phoebe's back has the same demure eyelet detailing as the front. Simple, elegant, and easy to wear, this top will add a touch of glitz to dressy or casual outfits. But it doesn't have to be a dressy piece. Phoebe would be cowgirl-cute in a denim-look yarn with woven gingham ribbon.

Phoebe

Skill level | INTERMEDIATE

Sizes

SMALL (Medium, Large, Extra-Large)
Instructions are given for smallest size, with
larger sizes in parentheses. When only one
number is given, it applies to all sizes.

Finished measurements

CHEST 37 (40, 42, 45)"/94 (101.5, 106.5, 114) cm
LENGTH 20½ (22, 22½, 24)"/52 (56, 57, 61) cm

Materials

3 (4, 5, 6) Lion Brand Yarn Glitterspun (60%
acrylic, 27% cupro, 13% polyester: 1¾ oz/50 g;
115 yds/105 m) in #153 Onyx

Needles

Size 9 (5.5 mm) or size needed to obtain gauge
Size G-6 crochet hook

Gauge

16 sts and 20 rows = 4"/10 cm over St st
To save time, take time to check gauge.

DESIGNER'S NOTES

*For those of us who are blessed with a waistline, on Phoebe I decreased and
increased a fourth time. But let's say you are knitting this for someone with a
Dolly Parton figure: You would start with the small size, work the decreases,
then increase up to the extra-large size and follow the sizing for the extra-
large. Then again, you have the option of following the armhole decreases back
to the smaller size.*

INSTRUCTIONS

front

With size 9 needles, CO 68 (74, 80, 86) sts.
Work even in St st until piece measures 3½
(4, 4, 5)"/7.5 (10, 10, 12.5) cm. Dec setup: K1,
place marker, k16, place marker, k to last 17
st, place marker, k16, place marker, k1. Dec
on RS 1 st after the first two markers and dec
1 st before the last two markers every 4th
row three times. Work even for 3 (3, 4, 4)"/7.5
(7.5, 10, 10) cm. Then inc 1 st after the first
two markers and inc 1 st before the last two
markers every 4th row three times. Work
until piece measures 13 (14, 14, 15)"/33 (35.5,
35.5, 38) cm.

SHAPE ARMHOLE: BO 3 sts at beg of
next 2 rows, then dec 1 st at each edge every
other row 4 (5, 5, 6) times 54 58, 64, 68) sts.
At the same time, work eyelet pattern:
Row 1: K3 * yo, k2tog, k4 * repeat * and end
by knitting leftover stitches. (You will be
shaping your armholes, so the number of sts
will change, and the number of knit stitches
here does not matter.)

Rows 2, 4, and 6: Purl.
Row 3: Knit.
Row 5: K1 *(yo, k2tog, k4)* ending with knit
stitches.
Repeat rows 1–6 for pattern. Work in pattern
until piece measures 17½ (19, 19½,
20)"/44.5 (48.5, 49.5 51) cm.
SHAPE NECK: Work 18 (20, 23, 25) sts.
Join a second ball of yarn and BO center 18
sts; work to end of row. Working both sides
at once, BO at each neck edge 4 sts once,
then dec 1 st every other row 3 times—11
(13, 16, 17) sts remaining each shoulder.
Work even until piece measures 20½ (22,
22½, 24)"/52 (56, 57, 61). BO.

back

Same as Front.

finishing

Sew shoulder and sides seams (see page 15).
With size G-6 hook, single crochet (see page
16) around neck and armholes.

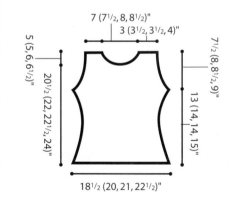

7 (7½, 8, 8½)"
3 (3½, 3½, 4)"
5 (5,6, 6½)"
7½ (8, 8½, 9)"
20½ (22, 22½, 24)"
13 (14, 14, 15)"
18½ (20, 21, 22½)"

lace all the way

Every knitter loves the lovely, finely patterned openwork designs of knitted lace. Light and airy, with a beautiful draping quality, knitted lace is not as difficult as it looks. The pretty eyelet patterns are formed by increasing, usually with yarn overs, and decreasing by knitting two stitches together, so that the number of stitches always remains the same. Here are two different lace patterns and three different sweater styles, offering an array of design possibilities.

This soft cotton tank is just a trifle flirty, with a beribboned empire waist setting off the open lace-patterned bottom from the stockinette-knit top. Pop it over a camisole and wear it under a jacket when the occasion is sedate, or show some midriff on a night out with friends.

Rebecca

Skill level | ADVANCED

Sizes

SMALL (Medium, Large, Extra-Large) Instructions are given for smallest size, with larger sizes in parentheses. When only one number is given, it applies to all sizes.

Finished measurements

CHEST 37 (40, 43, 46)"/94 (101.5, 109, 117) cm
LENGTH 22½ (24, 25½, 26)"/57 (61, 64, 66) cm

Materials

5 (6, 7, 8) skeins GGH Scarlett (100% cotton: 1¾ oz/50 g; 115 yds/105 m) in #35 Turquiose

Needles

Size 6 (4 mm) and size 10 (6 mm) straight and circular or size needed to obtain gauge

Gauge

19 sts and 24 rows = 4" /10 cm over St st, 15 sts and 18 rows = 4" /10 cm over St st
To save time, take time to check gauge.

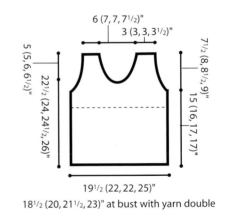

19½ (22, 22, 25)"
18½ (20, 21½, 23)" at bust with yarn double

DESIGNER'S NOTES

The lattice lace pattern is a little tricky but makes a good project for experienced knitters. For those less advanced knitters who love this flattering empire waistline design, you can substitute the easy lace pattern in Marta by adding a few stitches. For size small, CO 89 stitches, 99 stitches for medium, 109 stitches for large, and 119 stitches for extra-large. Then decrease to the number of stitches given for your size when you double the yarn.

INSTRUCTIONS

lattice-lace pattern

Multiple of 13 + 2

Row 1: K1, *k2, sl 1, k1, psso, k4, k2tog, k2, yo, k1, yo; repeat from * to last st, K1.

Row 2 and all even rows: Purl.

Row 3: K1, *yo, k2, sl 1, k1, psso, k2, k2tog, k2, yo, k3; repeat from * to last st, K1.

Row 5: K1, *k1, yo, k2, sl 1, k1, psso, k2tog, k2, yo, k4; repeat from * to last st, k1.

Row 7: K1, *yo, k1, yo, k2, sl 1, k1, psso, K4, k2tog, k2; repeat from * to last st, k1.

Row 9: K1, *k3, yo, k2, sl 1, k1, psso, k2, k2tog, k2, yo; repeat from * to last st, k1.

Row 11: K1, *k4, yo, k2, sl 1, k1, psso, k2tog, k2, yo, k1; repeat from * to last st, k1.

Repeat rows 1–12 for pattern.

front and back

With size 6 needles, CO 93 (106, 106, 119) sts. Work in pattern until piece measures 12 (13, 14, 14)"/30.5 (33, 35.5, 35.5) cm from beg, ending with wrong-side row. Change to size 10 needles and yarn double. Dec 25 (32, 26, 33) sts evenly across row—68 (74, 80, 86) sts. Continue in St st for 1"/2.5 cm, then on right-side row k1 *(k2tog, yo)* repeat end k1. Work until piece measures 15 (16, 17, 17)"/38 (40.5, 43, 43) cm.

SHAPE ARMHOLE: BO 3 sts at beg of next 2 rows, then dec 1 st at each edge every other row 4 (5, 6, 7) times.

SHAPE NECK: When piece measures 17 (18, 19, 19)"/43 (45.5, 48.5, 48.5) cm, work 16

Rebecca
(CONTINUED)

(19, 21, 22) sts. Join a second ball of yarn and BO center 18 (20, 20, 22) sts, work to end. Working both sides at once, BO at beg of each neck edge 2 sts 1 (1, 1, 2) times, then dec 1 st every other row 3 (4, 4, 4) times. Work even on remaining 11 (13, 14, 14) sts until armhole measures 7½ (8, 8½, 9)"/19 (20.5, 21.5, 23) cm. BO.

finishing

Sew shoulder and side seams (see page 15). Weave in drawstring ribbon.

NECK BAND: With size 10 circular needles and yarn double, pick up and knit 110 (114, 118, 122) sts around neck edge. Join and knit one row. BO all sts.

ARM BANDS: With RS facing, pick up 56 (62, 64, 66) sts evenly around armhole and knit 1 row. BO.

Kristina

You will love the luxurious feel and irresistible smoothness of this figure-flattering cashmere shell. Kristina uses the same lattice-lace pattern as Rebecca throughout the entire garment. Worn next to your body, it will feel like a second skin. But a complementary tank or cami underneath will showcase the openwork.

Skill level | ADVANCED

Sizes

SMALL (Medium, Large, Extra-Large)
Instructions are given for smallest size, with larger sizes in parentheses. When only one number is given, it applies to all sizes.

Finished measurements

CHEST 34 (39, 44, 50)"/86.5 (99, 112, 127) cm
LENGTH 20½ (22, 22½, 24)"/52 (56, 57, 61) cm

Materials

9 (10, 13) skeins Takhi Stacey Charles Filatura Di Crosa Cashmere (100% cashmere: 1¾ oz/ 50 g, 154 yds/140 m) in #06 Ecru

Needles

Size F-4 crochet hook
Size 6 (4 mm) or size needed to obtain gauge

Gauge

19 sts and 24 rows = 4"/10 cm over St st
To save time, take time to check gauge.

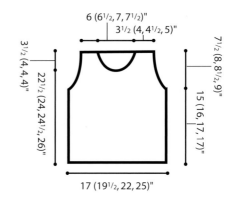

INSTRUCTIONS

lattice-lace pattern

Multiple of 13 + 2
Row 1: K1, *k2, sl 1, k1, psso, k4, k2tog, k2, yo, k1, yo; repeat from * to last st, k1.
Row 2 and all even rows: Purl.
Row 3: K1, *yo, k2, sl 1, k1, psso, k2, k2tog, k2, yo, k3; repeat from * to last st, k1.
Row 5: K1, *k1, yo, k2, sl 1, k1, psso, k2tog, k2, yo, k4; repeat from * to last st, k1.
Row 7: K1, *yo, k1, yo, k2, sl 1, k1, psso, k4, k2tog, k2; repeat from * to last st, k1.
Row 9: K1, *k3, yo, k2, sl 1, k1, psso, k2, k2tog, k2, yo; repeat from * to last st, k1.
Row 11: K1, *k4, yo, k2, sl 1, k1, psso, k2tog, k2, yo, k1; repeat from * to last st, k1.
Repeat rows 1–12 for pattern.

back

With size 6 needles, CO 80(93, 106, 119) sts. Work even in lattice-lace pattern until piece measures 15 (16, 17, 17)".
SHAPE ARMHOLE: BO 8 sts at beg of next

2 rows, then dec 1 st at each edge every other row 3 (5, 7, 9) times—58 (67, 76, 85) sts. Work even until piece measures 22½ (24, 24 26)"/57 (61, 61, 66) cm. BO loosely.

front

Work same as back until piece measures 19½ (21, 21, 23)"/49.5 (53.5, 53.5, 58.5) cm.
SHAPE NECK: Work 21(24, 23, 31) sts. Join a second ball of yarn and BO center 16 (19, 20, 23) sts; work to end of row. Working both sides at once, dec 1 st every other row 5 (6, 5, 7) times—16 (18, 18, 24) remaining sts for each shoulder. Work even until piece measures same as back. BO loosely.

finishing

Sew shoulder seams (see page 15).
NECK BAND: With F-4 crochet hook, single crochet and shrimp st around neck and armholes.
Sew on sleeves. Sew side and sleeve seams (see page 15).

Marta is an elegant tunic, knitted in an easy eight-row repeat lace pattern that's much less complex than it looks. Like Rebecca, an empire waist, subtly formed by omitting some of the lacework at the top, accents it. Notice the matching edges at the neckline, sleeves, and tunic bottom.

DESIGNER'S NOTES

This is a pattern that will give you several style options. Because the long sleeves are done in one straight piece, converting this to short sleeves or cap sleeves is a snap. You decide the length you want. You can also change the length of the body. Marta would be in the fashion forefront as either a hip-skimming sweater or a midriff-baring cropped top.

INSTRUCTIONS

lace pattern

Row 1: K1, k2tog, *k3, yo, k1, yo, k3, k3tog*, repeat to end k3, yo, k1, yo, k3, sl 1, k1, psso, k1.

Row 2 and all even rows: Purl.

Row 3: K1, k2tog, *k2, yo, k3, yo, k2, k3tog*, k2, yo, k3, yo, k2, sl1, k1, psso, k1.

Row 5: K1, k2tog, *k1, yo, k5, yo, k1, k3tog*, end k1, yo, k5, yo, k1, sl 1, k1, psso, k1.

Row 7: K1, k2tog, *yo, k7, yo, k3tog*, end yo, k7, yo, sl 1, k1, psso, k1.

Repeat rows 1–8 for pattern.

yoke pattern

Work center 23 (33, 23, 33) in lace, keeping remaining sts in St st.

back

With size 7 needles, CO 83 (93, 103, 113) sts. Work even in lace pattern until piece measures 21½ (22½, 22½, 23½)"/55 (57, 57, 59.5) cm. Start yoke pattern. Work 30 (30, 40, 40) sts in St st. Keep center 23 (33, 23, 33) sts in lace pat-tern, work remaining 30 (30, 40, 40) sts.

At the same time:

SHAPE ARMHOLE: When piece measures 22 (23, 23, 24)"/56 (58.5, 58.5, 61) cm, BO 5 sts at beg of next 2 rows, then dec 1 st at each edge every other row 5 (6, 8, 10) times—63 (71, 77, 83) sts. Work even until piece measures 29½ (31, 31½, 33)"/75 (79, 80, 84) cm. BO loosely.

front

Work same as back until piece measures 21½ (22½, 22½, 23½)"/55 (57, 57, 59.5) cm. Start yoke pattern. Work 30 (30, 40, 40) sts in St st. Keep center 23 (33, 23, 33) sts in lace pattern, work remaining 30 (30, 40, 40) sts. *At the same time:*

SHAPE ARMHOLE: When piece measures 22 (23, 23, 24)"/56 (58.5, 58.5, 61) cm, BO 5 sts at beg of next 2 rows, then dec 1 st at each edge every other row 5 (6, 8, 10) times—63 (71, 77, 83) sts. Start yoke pattern. Work

Skill level | INTERMEDIATE

Sizes

SMALL (Medium, Large, Extra-Large)
Instructions are given for smallest size, with larger sizes in parentheses. When only one number is given, it applies to all sizes.

Finished measurements

CHEST 35 (39, 43, 47)"/89 (99, 108, 119) cm
LENGTH 29½ (31, 31½, 33)"/75 (79, 80, 84) cm

Materials

Cascade Yarns Fixation (98.3% cotton/1.7% elastic 1¾ oz/50 g/186 yrds [stretched] 100 yds [relaxed])#8176 Ecru. *Note: If you use Fixation you may want to go up 2 needle sizes to obtain gauge.*

Needles

Size 7 (4.5 mm) straight and circular or size needed to obtain gauge

Gauge

19 sts and 24 rows = 4"/10 cm over St st
To save time, take time to check gauge.

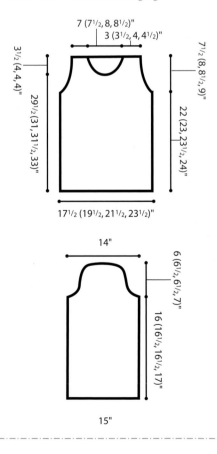

even until piece measures 26½ (28, 28½, 30)"/67 (71, 72, 76) cm.

SHAPE NECK: Work 21 (25, 28, 31) sts. Join a second ball of yarn and BO center 21 sts; work remaining 21 (25, 28, 31) sts. Working both sides at once, BO at each neck edge 4 sts once, then dec 1 st every other row 4 (4, 5, 6) times—13 (17, 19, 21) sts remaining for each shoulder. Work even until piece measures same as back. BO loosely.

sleeves

With size 7 needles, CO 73 (73, 73, 73) sts. Work in lace pattern until piece measures 16 (16½, 16½, 17)"/40.5 (42, 42, 43) cm.

SHAPE CAP: BO 5 sts at beg of next 2 rows. Then dec 1 st at each edge every other row 19 (19, 20, 21) times. Then BO 2 sts at beginning of next 4 rows. BO remaining 17 (17, 15, 13) sts.

finishing

Sew shoulder seams. Sew on sleeves. Sew side and sleeve seams. (See page 15 for details on sewing seams.)

NECK BAND: With circular needles, pick up and knit 83 sts around neck edge. Work rows 1–8 in lace pattern. BO all sts *loosely.*

intarsia & shape

This group of sweaters spotlights two design techniques. Fair Isle, a method for incorporating different colors in a knitted piece, involves knitting both colors at the same time to create colorful, intricate-looking patterns and stitches, as in the V-neck cardigan, Julia. Ursula and Tanya demonstrate how a knitted rectangle can turn into a fabulous garment, in both cases a shrug.

Those of you who are advanced knitters can really let your creativity shine and test your knitting skills by working side to side, alternating stitch patterns and yarns to create this gorgeous multitextured and many-colored V-neck cardigan. Choose a fun basket of five yarns of different colors and textures. Examples like red, black, white, silver, and ebony sparkle for a bold look. Or picture the five colors in hues of peaches and cream. Picking colors is almost as much fun as knitting them.

Julia

Skill level | ADVANCED

Sizes

SMALL (Medium, Large, Extra-Large)
Instructions are given for smallest size, with
larger sizes in parentheses. When only one
number is given, it applies to all sizes.

Finished measurements

CHEST 40 (44, 48, 56)"/101.5 (112, 122, 132) cm
LENGTH 25 (26, 27, 28)"/63.5 (66, 68.5, 71.5) cm

Materials

A: 9 (10, 12, 13) Plymouth Yarns Odyssey Glitz
(60% nylon, 37% wool, 3% lame: 1¾ oz/50 g;
66 yds/60 m) in #923

B: 2 (2, 3, 3) Berroco Yarns Zen (60% nylon,
40% cotton: 1¾ oz/50 g; 110 yds/100 m) in
#8219 Haiku Purple

C: 2 (3, 3, 3) Manos Del Uruguay Manos (100%
wool: 3.5 oz/100 g; 138 yds/126 m) in #F
Magenta

D: 3 (3, 4, 4) Knit One, Crochet Too, Inc.,
Tartelete (40% nylon, 50% cotton, 10% nylon:
1¾ oz/50 g; 75 yds/67 m) in #0647 Sea Jewels

E: 2 Takhi Stacy Charles Filatura Di Crosa Zara
(100% extra fine merino wool: 1¾ oz/50 g; 136
yds/125 m) in #1524 Brown

Needles

Size 10 (6 mm) and size 10.5 (6.5 mm) or size
needed to obtain gauge

Gauge

14 sts and 18 rows = 4"/10 cm over St st
To save time, take time to check gauge.

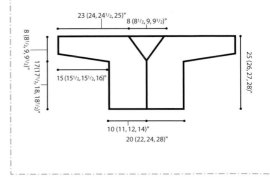

INSTRUCTIONS

pattern

Row 1: Knit A.

Row 2: Purl A.

Rows 3 and 7: *K3 A, k3 B* rep from*.

Rows 4 and 8: *K3 B, p3 A* rep from*.

Row 5: *K3 C, k3 A* rep from*.

Row 6: *P3 A, k3 C* rep from*.

Rows 9 and 11: Knit A.

Rows 10 and 12: Purl A.

Rows 13 and 14: Knit C.

Row 15: *K1 C, k1 D* rep from*.

Row 16: *K1 D, p1 C* rep from*.

Rows 17 and 18: Knit C.

Row 19: *K1 B, k3 A* rep from*.

Row 20: *P3 A, k1 B* rep from *.

Row 21: K1 A, *k1 C, k3 A * rep from *.

Row 22: P2 A, *k1 C, p3 A * rep from *.

Row 23: K2 A, *k1 C, k3 A * rep from *.

Row 24: P1 A, *k1 C, p3 A * rep from *.

Row 25: *K1 D, k3 A * rep from *.

Row 26: P1 D, *p1 A, p3 D * rep from *.

Row 27: Knit D.

Row 28: *P3 D, Bobble E*.

Row 29: Knit.

Row 30: P1 D, *p1 A, p3 D rep from *.

Row 31: K3* A, k1 D rep from *.

Row 32: Purl A.

Repeat rows 1–32 for pattern.

back

With size 10.5 needles and A, CO 84 (88, 92,
92) sts. Work pattern until piece measures 21
(23, 25, 26)"/53.5 (58.5, 63.5, 66) cm.

left front

With size 10.5 needles and A, CO 84 (88, 92,
92) sts. Work pattern until piece measures 7
(8, 9, 9½)"/18 (20.5, 23, 24) cm.

SHAPE NECK: BO 5 sts at each neck edge
every other row 9 (10, 10, 11) times. BO
remaining 29 (38, 42, 47) sts. Reverse shaping
for right front.

sleeves

With C and size 10.5 needles, CO 32 (34, 36,
36) sts.

Rows 1, 3, and 5: Knit.

Rows 2, 4, and 6: Purl.

Rows 7 & 8: Knit D.

Start pattern on Row 26. *At the same time,*
increase 1 st at each end every 4th row 14 (14,
15, 15) times, for 60 (62, 66, 66 sts). When
piece measures 15 (15½, 15½, 16)"/38 (39.5,
39.5, 40.5) cm, BO.

BOBBLE: On purl row: Turn, k1, p1, k1 in
same stitch, turn p3, turn, sl 1, k2tog, psso,
turn, purl this st with color D.

finishing

Sew shoulder, sleeves, and side seams (see
page 15).

BOTTOM BAND: With size 10 needles and C, pick up 172 (178, 186, 192) sts around bottom edge. Rows 1, 3, and 5: Purl. Rows 2 and 4: Knit. BO on Row 6.

NECK BAND: With size 10 needles and D, pick up 39 (41, 43, 43) sts up right front, 38 (40, 42, 42) sts along neck, 24 (24, 28, 28) sts across back, 38 (40, 42, 42) sts down neck edge, and 39 (41, 43, 43) sts down left front. 178 (186, 198, 198) sts. Work as follows:

Row 1: Purl D.

Row 2: Knit D.

Row 3: Bobble E, *p3D, Bobble E* rep from *.

Row 4: Knit D.

Row 5: Purl D.

Rows 6 and 7: Knit D.

Rows 8 and 10: Knit C.

Rows 9 and 11: Purl C.

Row 12: BO loosely in C.

Ursula

The shrug—what a versatile piece to come back into our wardrobes! Ursula might look intimidating, but the lace pattern is actually a long rectangle that's folded in half, then seamed from each side to form the sleeves. Ribbing along the edge of the opening left by the sleeves creates a flattering shawl collar in front and a tailored waist in back.

DESIGNER'S NOTES

This is an easy project for knitters of every level. Of course, the whole garment could simply be done in stockinette, but you could have a lot of fun doing a sampler of different stitches and not repeat one of them. This is just a rectangle, so let your imagination rule here.

INSTRUCTIONS

lace pattern
Row 1: K1, *k3, k2tog, yo, k1, yo, k2tog tbl, k2, rep from *, end k2.
Row 2 and all even rows: Purl.
Row 3: K1, * k2, k2tog, yo, k3, yo, k2tog tbl, K1, rep from *, end k2.
Row 5: K1, * k1, k2tog, yo, k5, yo, k2tog tbl, rep from *, end k2.
Rows 7, 9, and 11: K1, *p1, k2tog, k2, yo, k1, yo, k2, k2tog tbl, rep from *, end k2.
Row 13: K1, * k1, k2tog, yo, k5, yo, K2tog tbl, rep from *, end k2.

Row 15: K1, * k2, k2tog, yo, k3, yo, k2tog tbl, k1, rep from *, end k2.
Row 17: K1, *k3, yo, k2tog, k1, k2tog tbl, yo, k2, rep from *, end k2.
Row 19, 21, and 23: K1, * k1, yo, k2, k2tog, p1, k2tog tbl, k2, yo, * end k2.
Row 24: Purl.
Repeat rows 1–24 for pattern.

body
The body is one piece, worked cuff to cuff. With size 10½ needles, CO 53 sts and work in

lace pattern until piece measures 51 (53, 55, 57)"/128.5 (134.5, 140, 145) cm. BO all sts.

finishing
Fold in half lengthwise. Beginning at cuff, sew 15 (16, 16, 16)"/38 (40.5, 40.5, 40.5) cm under-arm seam, leaving a 21 (21, 23, 23)"/53.5 (53.5, 58.5, 58.5) opening.
With size 10½ circular needles, pick up 80 (80, 88, 88) sts along upper edge and 80 (80, 88, 88) sts along lower edge. Join work in K1, P1, ribbing for 3½"/9 cm. BO.

Skill level EASY

Sizes
SMALL (Medium, Large, Extra-Large) Instructions are given for smallest size, with larger sizes in parentheses. When only one number is given, it applies to all sizes.

Finished measurements
CHEST 18 (18, 19, 20)"/45.5 (45.5, 48.5, 51) cm
LENGTH 51 (53, 55, 57)"/128.5 (134.5, 140, 145) cm

Materials
8 (9, 10, 12) skeins Debbie Bliss Yarns Cash-merino Chunky (55% merino wool, 33% microfiber, 12% cashmere: 1¾ oz/50 g; 72 yds/64 m) in #09 Rose

Needles
Size 10.5 (6.5 mm) or size needed to obtain gauge

Gauge
14 sts and 17 rows = 4"/10 cm over St st
To save time, take time to check gauge.

51 (53, 55, 57)"

18 (18, 19, 20)"

Tanya

These fabulous shoes were the inspiration for Tanya, this little shrug with capped sleeves. Worked in the exotic-looking intarsia stitch pattern of Julia, it is constructed the same way as Ursula but from a smaller rectangle.

INSTRUCTIONS

body

With size 10½ needles, CO 53 (57, 61, 65) sts.

pattern

Row 1: Knit A.

Row 2: Purl A.

Rows 3 and 7: *K3 A, k3 B* rep from*.

Rows 4 and 8: *K3 B, p3 A* rep from*.

Row 5: *K3 C, k3 A* rep from*.

Row 6: *P3 A, k3 C* rep from*.

Rows 9 & 11: Knit A.

Rows 10 & 12: Purl A.

Rows 13 and 14: Knit C.

Row 15: *K1 C, k1 D* rep from*.

Row 16: *K1 D, p1 C* rep from*.

Rows 17 and 18: Knit C.

Row 19: *K1 B, k3 E* rep from*.

Row 20: *P3 E, k1 B* rep from*.

Row 21: K1 E, *k1 C, k3 E* rep from*.

Row 22: P2 E, *k1 C, p3 E* rep from*.

Row 23: K2 E, *k1 C, k3 E* rep from*.

Row 24: P1 E, *k1 C, p3 E* rep from*.

Row 25: *K1 D, k3 B* rep from*.

Row 26: P1 D, *p1 A, P3 D* rep from*.

Row 27: Knit D.

Row 28: *P3 D, Bobble E* rep from*.

Row 29: Knit.

Row 30: P1 D,* p1 B, p3 D* rep from*.

Row 31: *K3 B, k1 D* rep from*.

Row 32: Purl B.

Work in pattern until piece measures 26"/66 cm for cap sleeves, 36"/91 cm for short sleeves, 46"/117 cm for three-quarter-length sleeves, and 56"/142 cm for long sleeves. BO.

BOBBLE: On purl row: Turn, k1, p1, k1 into same stitch, turn, p3, turn, sl 1, k2tog, psso, turn. Purl this st with color D.

finishing

Fold in half and sew, leaving a 22"/56 cm opening. With D and size 10 circular needles, pick up 188 sts. Work K1, P1 ribbing for 3"/7.5 cm, working * 3 rows D, 1 row C *. Repeat from *. BO.

Skill level | INTERMEDIATE

Sizes

SMALL (Medium, Large, Extra-Large) Instructions are given for smallest size, with larger sizes in parentheses. When only one number is given, it applies to all sizes.

Finished measurements

CHEST 37 (40, 42, 45)"/94 (102, 107, 114)cm
LENGTH 20½ (22, 22½, 24)"/52 (56, 57, 60)cm

Materials

A: 1 (2, 2, 2) skeins Takhi Stacy Charles Collection Ritratto (28% mohair, 53% viscose, 10% polyamide, 9% polyester: 1¾ oz/50 g; 198 yds/180 m) in #85 Hazel

B: 2(2, 3, 3) skeins Berroco Yarns Zen (60% nylon, 40% cotton: 1 ¾ oz/50 g; 110 yds/100 m) in Blue

C: 1 (1, 1, 2) skeins Jade Sapphire Maju (100% silk: 1¾ oz/50g, 85 yds/78 m) in Blue

D: 4 (4, 5, 6) skeins Trendsetter yarns Pepita (86% polyamide, 14% polyester: 1¾ oz/50 g; 95 yds/87 m)

E: 2 (2, 3, 3) skeins Takhi Stacy Charles Tahki/Select Flower (25% sinflex, 35% tactlet, 40% polyester: 1¾ oz/50 g; 38 yds/35 m) in #010 Green

Needles

Size 10 (6 mm) circular and size 10½ (6.5 mm) or size needed to obtain gauge

Gauge

14 sts and 18 rows = 4"/10 cm over St st
To save time, take time to check gauge.

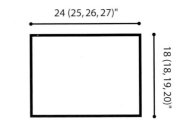

24 (25, 26, 27)"

18 (18, 19, 20)"

intarsia & shape **3**

List

OF ABBREVIATIONS

beg: beginning

BO: bind off

CC: contrasting color

cn: cable needle

CO: cast on

dec: decrease

inc: increase

k2tog: knit two together

MC: main color

psso: pass slipped stitch over

reverse St st: reverse stockinette stitch

sl: slip

st(s): stitch(es)

St st: stockinette stitch

tbl: through back loop

yo: yarn over

Resources

The yarns used in this book are widely available at fine yarn stores everywhere. We've offered this guide as a resource for locating the store nearest you.

Supplier names preceded by a + indicate that the website offers a store locator to make it easy to find the yarn you want quickly and easily.

Supplier names preceded by a * allow you to place online orders.

ARTEMIS SILK RIBBON

www.artemisinc.com
888-233-5187
Go to their website and fill out the online form for locations of retailers near you.
Dana, page 121

CASCADE YARNS

www.cascadeyarns.com
800-548-1048
1224 Andover Park E
Tukwila, WA 98188-3905
Marta (Fixation), page 139

BERROCO YARN

www.berroco.com
508-278-2527
14 Elmdale Road
P.O. Box 367
Uxbridge, MA 01569
Jacki (Optik), page 117; Julia (Zen), page 145; Tanya (Zen), page 151

+CRYSTAL PALACE YARNS

800-666-7455
www.straw.com
160 23rd Street
Richmond, CA 94804
Sandy (Chenille), page 61

Resources

CONTINUED

GREAT ADIRONDACK YARNS

www.yarnrep.com
516-843-3381
950 Co. Hwy 126
Great Adirondack, NY 12010

Ask your local yarn supplier for Great Adirondack Yarns.

Kenya (Cyclone), page 23; Camille (Frills & Sea Breeze), page 89; Dana (Caribe Irise), page 121

+JADE SAPPHIRE

www.jadesapphire.com
866-857-3897
At press time, the Jade Sapphire site did not have a complete listing of their yarns.

Ruby (Maju), page 27; Tanya (Maju), page 151

+KNIT ONE CROCHET TOO, INC.

www.knitonecrochettoo.com
207-892-9625
91 Tandberg Trail, Unit 6
Windham, ME 04062

Julia (Tartelete), page 145

+KNITTING FEVER

www.knittingfever.com
K.F.I.
516-546-3600
P.O. Box 336
315 Bayview Ave.
Amityville, NY 11701

Ursula (Debbie Bliss--Cash Merino Chunky), page 149

*LION BRAND YARN

www.lionbrandyarn.com
800-258-9276
Lion Brand Yarn
135 Kero Road
Carlstadt, NJ 07072

Eve (Cashmere Blend), page 21; Jessica (Incredible & Glitter Spun), page 39; Lynn (Wool-Ease) page 85; Susan (Wool-Ease: Thick and Quick), page 115; Phoebe (Glitter Spun), page 129

Resources

CONTINUED

MANOS DEL URUGUAY-- MANOS

Distributed by Design Source Distribution
888-566-9970
PO Box 770
Medford, MA 02155

Manos Del Uruguay is distributed by Design Source Distribution and is available in most fine yarn shops. Call the number listed above to get the name of a shop near you.

Julia (Manos), page 145

+MUENCH YARNS

www.muenchyarns.com
800-733-9276
1323 Scott St.
Petaluma, CA 94954

Muench Yarns' website also has an order form that you can download to order by mail or by fax.

Paula (GGH Velour), page 49; Elizabeth (GGH Samoa), page 73; Rebecca (GGH Scarlett), page 133

+PLYMOUTH YARN Co.

www.plymouthyarn.com
215-788-0459
P.O. Box 28
Bristol, PA 19007

Sara (Electra), page 59; Terri (Odyssey Glitz), page 81; Cece (Fantasy Naturale), page 101; Julia (Odyssey Glitz), page 145

+PRISM ARTS

www.prismyarn.com
3140 39th Ave North
St. Petersburg, FL 33714

Tracy (Wild Stuff), page 47; Suki (Cool Stuff & Bon Bon), page 55; Leah (Flash), page 107

Resources

CONTINUED

can n
fron
addin
trastin
i
pat
bro
ter
st
bru
r
r

*+TAHKI STACY CHARLES

www.tahkistacycharles.com
800-338-9276
Tahki Stacy Charles, Inc.
70-30 80th St. Building 36
Ridgewood, NY 11385

Kenya (Millefili Fine), page 23; Madonna, page 65 (Venus & Cotton Classic; Sheila, page 69 (Venus); Anne, page 79 (Crosa Millefili Fine & Cancun); Mary (Posh), page 97; Cecilia (Victoria), page 103; Judy (Baby tweed), page 111; Kristina (Cashmere), page 137; Julia (Zara), page 145; Tanya (Ritratto & Flower), page 151

+TRENDSETTER YARNS

www.trendsetteryarns.com
800-446-2425
16745 Saticoy St. Suite 101
Van Nuys, CA 91406

Ruby (Flora), page 27; Elizabeth (Dune), page 73; Jackie (Dune), page 117; Tanya (Pepita), page 151

UNIQUE KOLOURS LTD.

www.uniquekolours.com
800-252-3934
28 N. Bacton Hill Rd.
Malvern, PA 19355

Goldi, page 33; Goldilocks (Colinette Giatto), page 35

+ WESTMINSTER FIBERS

www.knitrowan.com
800-445-9276
4 Townsend West, Unit 8
Nashua, NH 03063

Westminster Fibers is the U.S. distributor of Rowan yarns. The address provided is for Westminster Fibers. The website will take you to Rowan.

Katherine (Kid Silk Haze), page 43; Emily (Cotton Rope), page 93; Victoria (Kid Silk Haze), page 125

½ (4,4,4)

20½ (22, 22½, 24)

3½ (4,4,4)

20½ (22, 22½, 24)

Index

C O N T I N U E D

About the Author

Melissa Matthay spent twenty years as owner and operator of The Yarn Co. in New York City—rated "Best of New York," before moving her knits and her family to Madison, Wisconsin. There she brought her enthusiasm to the charming and popular Knitting Tree. She has also been featured on DIY's *Knitty Gritty* and in *Family Circle Easy Knitting*. Recently, Melissa has taken time off from the yarn retail business, instead devoting all her time to designing garments for magazines and for upcoming books for Potter Craft.

Knits Three Ways is Melissa Matthay's eighth publication. Also under her knitting belt are: *Perfectly Brilliant Knits* (Martingale and Company 2005), *Knitting Patterns by Melissa: v.1 Babies to Toddlers* (Melissa Matthay 2005), *Knitting Patterns by Melissa: v.2 Toddlers to Tots* (Melissa Matthay 2005), *Little Box of Scarves* (Martingale and Company 2004), *Little Box of Sweaters* (Martingale and Company 2004), *Little Box of Scarves 2* (Martingale and Company 2004), and *Basically Brilliant Knits* (Martingale and Company 2003).

se three sweaters, although

rent styles, have one thi

on: The tank, the long-s

, and the sleeveless she

nitted using the same int

g stitch pattern, which

acy squares that res

Everyone loves

cardigan

an

or so

your gi

Katherine, re

...ese three sweaters, althou...

...thing in common: The ta...

...weater, and the sleeveless...

...itted using the same intri...

...stitch pattern, which fe...

...ours of lacy squares that...

...ables broomstick-lace...

Everyone k...

...ong

...hand...

attention...

...proper; the rib...